THE COLLEGE ADMISSIONS PLAN SIMPLIFIED

A BUSY PARENT'S P.L.A.N. TO A DEBT-FREE DEGREE

SHELLEE HOWARD

Copyright © 2024 College Ready

All rights reserved. No part of this book may be reproduced or transmitted in any form or by any means, electronic or mechanical, including photocopying, recording, or by any information storage and retrieval system, without written permission of the author, except for the inclusion of brief quotations in a review.

Cover Design by: Zeljka Kojic

ISBN: 979-8-218-55178-0 (paperback)

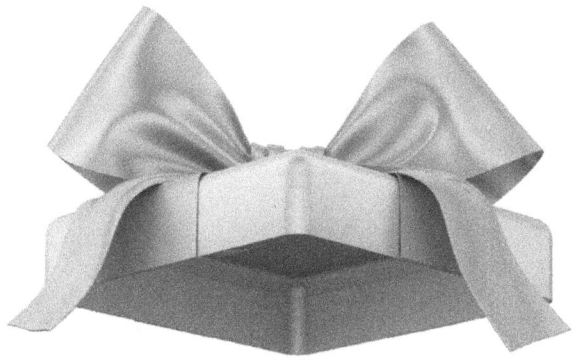

Free gift

P = **PLAN FOR YOUR CHILD'S ACADEMIC POSITIONING.** - Timeline for Success.
L = **LEARN WHAT YOUR CHILD IS PASSION ABOUT** - 100 Community Service Ideas.
A = **APPLYING TO COLLEGE:** - Crafting a Winning College Application.
N = **NEGOTIATE: COLLEGE IS A BUSINESS** - 10 Secrets to Scholarships.

Resources will be updated quarterly
http://collegereadyplan.com/bookresources

Table of Contents

Acknowledgments 1

About the Author 3

My Story 5

P = Plan: Plan for Your Child's Academic Positioning 9

Parent's Corner 11

My Gift to You 13

Chapter 1 – Planning For College: Why It Really Matters 17

Chapter 2 – What Is Most Important to Your Family –
Academic Fit, Social Fit, Talent Fit, or Financial Fit
(Do You Want or Need Scholarships) 29

Chapter 3 – If You Are Planning for a Top Tier Education,
You Must Start Planning Now 33

L = Learn: Learn What Your Child Is Passionate About 37

Chapter 4 – Learn How Passion With a Purpose is Not the
Same as Community Service 39

Chapter 5 – Learn How to Help Your Child Stand Out and
How to Position Them for Success:
The Top 3 Things Colleges Are Looking For 43

Chapter 6 – Learn How To Evaluate The ROI of College:
Can Your Family Afford College? Can Your Student Afford
Not To Go To College? 55

A = Apply: Applying to College: The Application, Leadership, Extracurriculars, Recommenders and Essays 67

Chapter 7 – Apply a Timeline for Success: What Should You
and Your Child Do, and When Should They Do It? 69

Chapter 8 – Applying: A Standout Application 93

Chapter 9 – Applying Your Plan to Crush the Interviews and Get Off The Waitlist 105

N = Negotiate: College is a Business —Do Not Pay Full Price 109

Chapter 10 – Valuable Lessons and How to Negotiate: What You Don't Know is Costing You (SAI/FAFSA/CSS) 111

Chapter 11 – Negotiate to Get Big Scholarships – Build a Strategic List of Generous Colleges 131

Chapter 12 – Finances: College Without Student Loans – Negotiate 143

Quick PLAN for Parents 159

Final Thoughts 167

Next Steps 169

Glossary 189

Acknowledgments

This book is dedicated to my two oldest children, Ryan and Makena. My husband Mark and my two stepchildren Noah and Annika. My Italian exchange student Bella and my Ugandan friends Brinda and Yona who have shown me the importance of inspiring children all over the world. You all inspire me every day to be the best I can be. Without you, this book would never have been written. Your desire to help others inspired me to write this book, and your support and accountability helped me finish it. You are all a true testament that living your passion on purpose not only changes your life but other people's lives all over the world as well. Keep living your dream, and I hope to inspire other children to find their passion and never give up on what they want.

To my parents, who taught me at an early age that I could do anything if I wanted it badly enough. The gift of tenacity has helped me throughout my life. Your love and support helped me be confident enough to be the first in our family to go to college.

To my College Ready team, I am so fortunate to have the opportunity to work with each of you. You are impacting the lives of teenagers all over the world, and I am so grateful for your endless support and dedication to our mission of helping one million families get into college and graduate with minimal debt.

A special thank you to the many families who have hired me and trusted me with their children's futures. I have learned so much from each student I have had the honor of working with. I will always treasure the laughter and the tears, but most of all, the grateful hugs and thank you testimonials I have received from your children.

Introduction

Harvard Graduation 2016

Student loan debt has just reached an all-time high, amounting to $1.6 trillion dollars![1] Young adults are getting out of college with tens of thousands of dollars in debt that they can't pay off while supporting themselves. Many have had to move back in with their parents to make ends meet. It's a terrible problem that families are struggling with.

I wrote this book to help you gain the knowledge needed and teach you that it is possible to go to college and graduate without debt. In this book, I am going to show you exactly how your child can go to the college of their dreams without paying full price and, in many cases, even get out of

---

[1] According to recent data, the total student loan debt in the United States is currently around $1.6 trillion, with the source being the Federal Reserve, which tracks consumer credit data including student loans; this figure indicates a record high for student loan debt.

college debt-free. You'll also discover my top tips on how to create a successful application, why your child can afford to go to college, and the secrets of free money and scholarships. This book will prevent you from making costly mistakes that many families make. I'd like to start by introducing myself and telling you how I came to be an Independent College Consultant and expert in college admissions and financial strategist.

About the Author

My name is Shellee Howard, and I am the founder and CEO of College Ready (College Admissions), CR Future Now (Career Exploration), and University Ready (Study Abroad). I am a certified independent college admissions consultant, financial college strategist, and career counselor. I am an international speaker and award winner. I have been featured on FOX, CBS, and NBC and am the author of the best-selling book, "How to Send Your Student to College Without Losing Your Mind or Your Money."

We help middle and high school students (and their parents) by preparing them for their future. We help them find their "why," gifts, talents, passions, and core values, find the perfect career, and teach them the path to take for financial success. For students who wish to pursue college, we help them create a standout strategy while striving for the best academic, social, athletic, and financial fit. I am a 5th generation from OC, California, and I enjoy inspiring teenagers worldwide.

I am passionate about various causes, both privately and through my 3rd world outreach projects. Currently, I am building a school in Uganda for 800+ children, providing education opportunities in Oaxaca, and engaging in other humanitarian efforts. When not working, you will find me traveling internationally and serving those in need, where I have visited over 91 countries.

My Story

I was the first child on both sides of my family to go to college; I had no guidance but a lot of determination. I graduated from college in four years despite changing my major five times because I attended summer school and winter sessions. I made so many costly mistakes that I promised myself that my children would not make them, too. Instead, they would have a bulletproof plan.

Four days after I graduated from college, I started working in sales for Procter and Gamble and was fortunate to go through all their first-class training programs. I climbed right through the corporate ceiling in eight years. After having my children, I dedicated myself to being the best mom I could be while still working full-time. Fast forward to my son's 8th grade year, and my story becomes more interesting… In the spring semester of my son's 8th-grade year, he came home from school and informed me that he had picked his high school classes and had decided that he would like to be a brain surgeon. I felt the pressure immediately; I had no idea how to help him! I started with his soon-to-be high school counselor, who asked, "Why would you want to go to school for that long and incur so much debt?" I realized at that moment that I was on my own. Feeling defeated, I put on my "mom" face and told him I would take care of it and just stay focused on getting good grades and finding his passion. Fast forward to his senior year in high school. Not only did my son listen to everything that I advised, but he also worked the plan I built for him. He applied to twelve universities, half of which were Ivy schools. Of those, he was accepted into eleven, and out of eleven, he received offers for a free education at half of them. After his list of acceptances was announced, I had people calling me and asking for a plan and advice.

At that point, I went back to college and got my college counseling certification from UCSD. After completing my certification, I founded College Ready LLC 2008, CR Future Now 2020, and University Ready 2022. We have helped over 15,000 students prepare for college admission. 75% of our clients come from referrals. 93% of our students got into their top three schools. Over the last three years, our students have earned over $23 million in scholarships! Our goal is to help your family achieve your goal. Whether your child is aiming for the Ivy League, other private institutions, state universities, or small liberal arts colleges, our experts are here to guide your family to a college that's right for them.

Since writing my first book, my son graduated from Harvard debt-free, took a gap year and was hired by Bain Consulting, decided to apply to medical school, and attended the University of California, San Diego. From there, he graduated with only $30,000 in total loans and is completing his final year as an Orthopedic Surgery Resident at the University of California Los Angeles. My son will be able to pay off all his college loans in his first year as a surgeon. That is a fantastic ROI! My daughter was accepted at her dream school, the University of Alabama, and she graduated from CBU with an RN degree. She is a full-time Pediatric Registered Nurse with zero debt. This allowed her to buy her first home at 25 years old. This is just a snapshot of my journey. I have helped thousands of families all over the world get into and graduate from the college of their dreams with little to no debt. Desire is the key. If your student has it.... with planning and strategy, they will obtain it! Every student is unique and comes with gifts, talents, and opportunities. I work with families to create a plan that allows their students to stand out and shine among their competition.

My proven "PLAN" strategy is successful with all students. We focus on the student first, set the goal, and then create their custom plan. There is a perfect college waiting for your child, and I will help you find it. What you don't know will cost you both time and money. Take, for example, a student (client) of mine, Michael. Michael came to me as a freshman and had no idea where he wanted to go to college or what he wanted to major in. He had a strong GPA but wasn't in the most challenging classes. He had not done any test prep but tested well on his first PSAT. He enjoyed doing community service but was more of a follower than a leader. In just three short years, Michael will graduate this Spring with nine college offers to choose from. Several of his choices will allow him to attend debt-free. Having a plan, Michael was not overwhelmed by the process. He followed the College Ready PLAN and adjusted along the way. He now knows his dream college and major, but more importantly, he knows what he wants to do after he graduates from college because we took the time to help Michael grow in all areas of his life. There are a lot of stories just like Michael's from students who graduated from college in four years debt-free because they used our PLAN. You and your student can be one of these success stories…but only if you plan and if you start now. College is more competitive and expensive than it has ever been. How will you plan for your child's success?

If your son or daughter is only a freshman or in middle school, you may be thinking that you have "plenty of time." Nothing could be further from the truth. Many of my clients have been with me since the summer before high school. They started their college plans from day one of high school, allowing them to be stress-free and not make any costly mistakes.

If your son or daughter is a sophomore, junior, or senior, it is not too late, but if you want the big scholarships, timing is critical. The longer you wait to plan, the more college will cost your family. Reading this book will show you how NOT to make the costly mistakes so many families do. It will give you knowledge about college admission as well as the costs of college. I promise you that after you read this book, you will be armed with the knowledge and tools you need so your child can pay as little as possible to attend college.

If you do not have time to read the whole book, I have created a "Quick PLAN for Parents" section at the back of the book. You can always start there and then read one section a day for 12 days, and you will have the knowledge to not make mistakes.

Everyone I meet asks me the same thing....
"Where do I start"?

Start here: Who will be responsible for completing (check all boxes)?

Essential Steps	Parent will take the lead	Child possesses the skills	Need Professional Assistance
Academic Strategy			
Financial Strategy			
Test Strategy			
Leadership Strategy			
Extra Curricular Strategy			
Recommender Strategy			
Essay Strategy			
Passion with Purpose Strategy			
Strength & Career Assessments			

THERE ARE MANY MORE, BUT THIS SHOULD GET YOU STARTED

For additional Essential Steps, refer to the
Quick PLAN for Parents section at the back of this book.

P = Plan:
Plan for Your Child's Academic Positioning

Parent's Corner

I wrote this book for you, the parent. So much about College Admissions is written to help the student. What about the parent? What is your role in all of this? As parents, we sometimes become utterly exhausted trying to help our children—no matter their age. Understanding everything your child needs to be successful and helping them be prepared can be overwhelming. As a mom of five, I can completely relate. I see you and hear you!

The late nights spent worrying, the difficult conversations, the endless support you give your child even when it feels like you're running on empty. Raising a middle school, high school, or college student is a journey filled with highs and lows, and I want you to know that your efforts are seen and they matter more than you might realize.

Your child is navigating one of the most challenging and transformative times of their life. They are growing, learning, and sometimes struggling to find their way. It's not easy, and it's certainly not always smooth. But in these moments of uncertainty, your presence and your belief in them are more powerful than any advice or solution.

Remember that brain development continues into the mid-20s. Your child is still growing and still learning how to manage their emotions, make decisions, and understand the world around them. It may seem like they've got it all figured out, or it may seem like they're lost, but either way, they still need you. They need your guidance, your wisdom, and most importantly, your unwavering support.

My Gift to You

Today, I was reading a news article and found some information I thought you should know. This year, Vanderbilt announced they will be raising tuition again. The total yearly cost will be over $100,000![2]

Fifteen years ago, this school was on my son's college list. He was accepted with a massive scholarship and honestly considered attending there until USC offered a full ride, and Harvard matched it. Yes, Harvard for FREE!

As I reflect on the last 18 years that I have owned College Ready, it still frustrates me that some students get a ton of money, and others do not even know where to find it. This will be my 18th year helping families apply for college. I am looking forward to our rising Senior kick-off meeting and feel so proud of our student's success in 2023. With no help from the FAFSA, our Seniors earned over $7.2 million in scholarships this year. We know where to find the money, and it is my mission to help families just like yours get into the best-fit college and graduate with as little debt as possible.

My first-born son did not have a perfect GPA or test score, but he was accepted to Harvard pre-med (regenerative Biology) and seven other top-tier colleges. He graduated in four years debt-free! Everyone wants to know how he did it... He used the same strategy I teach today. The same one my daughter used to get into the University of Alabama on a full-ride scholarship. The same one my stepson used to get into SFSU and was able to get out in three years debt-free. The College Ready plan even worked

---

[2] According to a report from the New York Times, the source for the information that Vanderbilt's total yearly cost will exceed $100,000 is a recent announcement from the university regarding a tuition increase, with some students potentially facing a total cost exceeding $100,000 when considering room, board, and other fees for the 2024-2025 academic year

for my stepdaughter, who is attending AAU in Prague, where she will get a US and European business degree in three years for $27,000. She is working her way through college so she will graduate debt-free. My children are not any different than your children. College Ready has helped thousands of students get into college and graduate without debt. It is possible, and we want to help you accomplish the same thing!

Even if you can write a check for $400,000, wouldn't it be great to use that money for a down payment on your child's first home? That is exactly what I did, and it felt fantastic for my son to earn his way through college. He now has the determination and tenacity to get through life. Scholarships are not just for those who can't afford college tuition; scholarships are available to any student willing to do the work.

There are three types of scholarships: institutional, independent, and need-based. There is more money available than you can fathom. Billions of dollars are gifted every year, so why not your family? Strategy is the key to success. You need a strategy to get your children into college, and you need a strategy to pay for it. You need to understand the process and know what steps to take to ensure your child receives what they deserve for their hard work.

I started each of my children's strategies when they picked their very first classes in high school. Their test strategy gave them huge scholarships, and their community service strategy got them accepted into their dream schools and provided huge scholarships. Their leadership set them apart from their competition, their letters of recommendation came from congressmen and women, and their essays got them accepted into eleven colleges with huge scholarships. Together, all their scholarships equaled full rides. It was not easy, but it was possible. No one could believe it when my second child also received a full ride.

My oldest son is turning 30 next month and is finishing his medical residency at UCLA. Soon, he will start his fellowship with a total of $30,000 in subsidized loans, which he will pay off in his first year as a surgeon. My oldest daughter is an RN with no debt and was able to buy her first home by herself at 25 years old. I do not share this to boast; I share it to show that it is possible even in Orange County, California. Social media says it is not possible, and we have proven year after year that it is.

If you are feeling overwhelmed, discouraged, frustrated, confused, or do not know where to start or how to help your child, please reply to this email, and I am happy to share exactly what our students have been doing over the last 17 years to get into college and graduate with minimal debt.

We can help your child if they are in 8th through 12th grade. Once you accept a college, your scholarship chances decrease drastically. However, picking the correct college list and knowing how to negotiate financial aid can help you get scholarships no matter how much you make.

Please do not leave this process up to your 16-year-old; they have no idea what this kind of debt can do to their future. They need you and a village of wise professionals to help them get into college, stand out, and get the big money.

As a thank you for reading this entire message, I would like to offer your child a gift. Our College Ready students have created a passion with purpose project that is completely free to join. It is by invitation only. Go to www.collegereadyplan.com/quickplan to receive a link to our weekly meeting where students from all over the world work together to make our world a better place for children who dream of an education.

With gratitude,
Shellee Howard
CEO/Founder of College Ready

Chapter 1

Planning For College: Why It Really Matters

We plan for marriage, for children, to buy a car and a home, and for retirement, yet very few families have a plan for their child's future. I have met with thousands of families over the last 17 years, and most of them fall into one of these four categories:

How families PLAN for College admissions

DENIAL | PUT YOUR HEAD IN THE SAND | DO IT YOURSELF | USE EXPERTS

Which one are you currently in? Do you have a plan? Years ago, families started planning for college during their junior or senior year of high school. It was less competitive and less expensive then. Everyone wants to know the secret to my children's success; it's simple: we started planning their future in preschool. I did not say that we started planning for college then, but we did talk about college as part of their future. Even if they chose not to attend college, I wanted them to feel in control of their future and know all their options. We visited colleges on family trips like we did museums, monuments, art galleries, and science exhibits. We would walk around the campus and talk about fond memories of college, and even eat on campus when possible. My goal was to give my children exposure to all their options and make college a reality if that is what they ultimately chose. By the time my oldest was in third grade, I had a good idea of the kind of student he would be. I taught him to enjoy all types of reading. I read so he would want to read. During his middle school years, I taught him the joy of serving those less fortunate. I exposed him to leadership and foreign languages.

Middle school is the best time for our children to explore new things and test their abilities. This will give them the confidence in high school to lead others to do the same. All my children were given opportunities to explore their world safely while also allowing for some small failures. The goal was to help them learn about who they are and the gifts they were given to explore their strengths and challenge their abilities.

The gift of tenacity is something children need to be successful in life. The real planning started in 8th grade for all my children, and it is the best time for your child as well. The classes they take in 8th grade will set them up for the best path in high school and beyond. Taking a class in leadership, music, foreign language, or something that gets them looking forward to going to school will be important as they face the challenges of navigating high school. Middle school is the time to utilize tutors and take challenging classes. The summer between middle school and high school is the most underutilized summer for most students.

Unfortunately, most families do not realize that as soon as your child is promoted from 8th grade, the college clock starts ticking. So, instead of phone time, computer time, and game time, I encouraged all my children to find a passion and start exploring things they wish to see change in the world. Explore future careers, talk to friends and family about their careers, and get clarity on what brings them joy.

The college application starts the day your child is promoted from 8th grade; this is the best time to start planning for college. If you are reading this book and have a freshman, sophomore, junior, or senior in high school, it's not too late. But the earlier you start, the easier the process will be, and the bigger the scholarships!

PLANNING FOR COLLEGE: WHY IT REALLY MATTERS

What do you want your child's future to look like? What do they want? If they currently do not know, what is your plan to help them?

To receive a list of the most important questions to ask your child and gain clarity for their future, visit www.collegereadyplan.com/quickplan

The secret weapon that parents use to send their children to college without losing their minds or their money is having a College PLAN. Let's start by giving you the knowledge that will help you plan to be College Ready.

So, your child has decided they would like to go to college. Congratulations! You must be so excited and proud of their decision. For some parents, this process may be scary, overwhelming, and possibly dreadful if they did not go to college or they attended University in another country. As a parent and strategic college admissions counselor, I will guide you and your child on a path to a successful college application season.

If you attended college more than ten years ago, you will be surprised at how much the process has changed and the costs have increased. I understand any apprehensive feelings about the application process or how to help position your child for success. After decades, my experience with thousands of college applications has prepared me to help you. Because every family is unique and every child comes with unique gifts and talents, I thought this illustration might help you understand that even in my own family, my children took different paths.

Child #1: Had a plan we started in 8th grade: Got accepted to Harvard in 2012 (dream school), graduated debt-free in 2016 with a biology degree, worked at Bain Consulting for one year, got accepted into UCSD medical school in 2017, and then was matched with UCLA Orthopedic Residency in 2021. Next year, he will start his final fellowship.

Child #2: Had a plan we started in 7th grade: Got accepted to the University of Alabama in 2016 (dream school), graduated debt-free in 2021, and is currently an RN working in the best pediatric emergency room in California.

Child #3: Did not want a plan and thought he could do it on his own. During the application season of his senior year in high school, he came to us wishing he had planned. We were able to come up with a quick plan, and he was accepted into San Francisco State University. He was still able to graduate with a major and a minor in 2024, debt-free.

Child #4: Did not want to follow a "normal plan." My stepdaughter applied to college in 2022 and will graduate with a dual US and European International Business Degree in three years from AAU in Prague debt-free.

Child #5: My Italian exchange student daughter applied to The Farm University in Venice, Italy, in 2022 and will graduate in three years.

I'm sharing this information with you to show that even in my own family, each of my children had their own goals and dreams. With their unique positioning and a perfect strategy for success, all five will graduate debt-free, and I did not pay a penny!

There is one thing parents have in common: they fear messing up their child's college application, and they lose sleep worrying about how they will pay for college.

I quickly learned that the college application process is nothing like it used to be. Gone are the good old days when you could:

- Pay your way into a college.

- Take one standardized test—just one time—and submit one score.

- Attend community college while figuring out your major, get your AA in two years, and transfer to a university to finish your degree in four years.

- Pre-register for classes and get the classes you want.

- Work and pay for your own college education.

- Get into a college based on your GPA alone.

- Get a full-ride scholarship plus housing to play a sport.

So much has changed in just 20 years. Remember that applying to college is competitive, and you should take the process seriously. The time your child puts into the college application process will be worth the effort. Do not assume anything as you educate yourself on your child's options. What you do not know in this process will cost you and your child. I encourage you to speak with your child about who will create the plan and who will hold your child accountable. Do not assume your child will get the help they need from their high school or college. Do not assume that your teenager can do this on their own. Do not assume Google is the answer. The sooner you have the "money" discussion, the better for all involved.

When Should Your Student Start Preparing for College?

This is one of the top five questions I get when speaking to a large audience. The answer is quite simple: You should start when your child is ready and shows interest. In my line of work, I often encounter many people who are interested in my son's journey to Harvard. As soon as someone finds out that my son got into Harvard and graduated in four years debt-free, they want to know the secret! I hate to be the bearer of bad news, but there is no secret. Good behaviors, habits, hard work, and passion are what will lead your student to a dream school. After being a Certified Independent College Consultant for more than seventeen years, I have seen a pattern emerge in the students who are successful in getting into the college of their dreams, such as:

- **Teach your child to love reading and knowledge from an early age.** I am not suggesting that you become obsessive about a toddler's education. However, an early introduction to books they enjoy can greatly impact their future. You can also be an example as a reader yourself. Read to them; when they are old enough, have them read to you. This may sound simple, but establishing a love for learning will help them enjoy school all the way through college.

- **Talk to your child about your college experience and your alma mater.** Tell them stories about how much you enjoyed college. This will set the tone for future conversations and questions about college.

- **When you are on a family vacation, take a half-day and tour a nearby college.** Let your child see what college life is like and why it is important for them to attend college. College is not for everyone, but at the early stages of childhood, sharing knowledge is the key to having options. Personal enjoyment of education and learning will happen at different times for each child. If you have a child who enjoys learning, then I suggest you put them into a college prep school or the GATE program at a public school. The goal is to keep the child challenged and to enjoy learning. The key here is not to push or force the child but to support and guide them. Balance is the key to a lifetime of learning. Pursuing passions is a huge part of preparing to go to college. Most children will show interest in particular hobbies at a young age, and it is important to expose them to various activities. Timewise, most children will know their gifts and talents by middle school.

- **Continue to encourage your child to try new things.** Their classes in middle school will set them up for their high school academic experience. Seek some academic support as soon as you realize your child may need help in one subject or across the curriculum. It is unrealistic to think that if your child struggles in math, they will be allowed to take the more challenging math classes in high school. Your child will be tested along the way, and these test scores will be used to determine where your child will be placed in high school. If your child is struggling in one subject, getting a tutor as soon as possible is recommended. Math, for example, is a building block. If a child struggles in pre-algebra, they will find Algebra 1 and Algebra 2 very difficult. Always make sure your child master's the fundamentals before moving on too quickly. In English, the same can be true. If a child struggles with sentence structure, they will not want to write essays in high school and college. This may seem fundamental, but this is where many parents make mistakes when shaping their children's schedules. Pushing a child to move on to the next level too quickly will stress out the child and can cause future problems.

- **A child's college application starts in eighth grade.** Your child will not need to list all eighth-grade classes or grades. However, be aware that your child can take high school level classes in middle school. These courses are like a gateway; they will allow children to start high school at an advantage. Taking advanced math, English, and foreign language classes are ways to get ahead. If your child takes pre-algebra in 8th grade, they will get to start algebra in high school, etc. Every class counts!

COLLEGE READY CASE STUDY: Preparing to Succeed

Let me share a true story about two students who attended two different middle schools but the same public high school. The first student, Jackie, attended a private elementary and middle school; she transferred to a public high school in 9th grade. The second student, Brian, attended a public middle school and the same public high school as Jackie. Jackie had the opportunity to take pre-Algebra and Spanish 1 in middle school, so she started high school in Algebra 1 and Spanish 2. Brian also took pre-Algebra, but he was not able to take a foreign language because he chose to be in leadership at his middle school. Brian started high school in Algebra 1 and Spanish 1.

No AP or IB classes were offered at their school during their freshman year. Both students continued to take the most challenging schedule of classes that were offered at their school. Both Jackie and Brian received As in every high school class they took. During the final week of their senior year, the class ranking was announced, which is when reality set in. Jackie was announced as the valedictorian, and Brian was the salutatorian. The difference between 1st in their class and 2nd in their class was starting with Spanish 1 vs. Spanish 2.

The happy ending here is that both students went on to the colleges of their dreams, but this real-life example is meant to show the importance of class selection and planning. Getting into college today is challenging and costly. Not planning properly could cause your child to miss out on college acceptances and scholarship money.

So, where does your child begin? As stated before, 8th graders need to consider their high school schedule. The college application starts with the listing of the first high school classes. Every schedule—from the fall of their freshman year—to the spring of their senior year is very important. Every student must complete all courses necessary to graduate from high school. There is a list of classes that every student must take, and then there are classes that colleges require. Knowing this information before planning a high school schedule is critical to the results.

Many high schools hold orientations for incoming freshmen in the spring. Please do not leave class schedule planning to your 14-year-old child! Many children will pick easy classes, classes with their best friends, and classes that sound fun. Your involvement is critical at this point. The high school may tell your child they are not smart enough for a class or that the class is already full. Your child may be told that they should take a certain class next academic year. It is critical that you be an advocate for your child. Children have been taught to respect their elders, so when adults tell them no, they often accept the no. More than 50% of the students I mentor have dealt with this situation in some fashion. Parents may need to be an advocate for their child if necessary.

As a parent, I had to sit down with my children's high school administration every semester. I understand high schools deal with thousands of students and have guidelines and rules. However, I will never understand why the interest of the child does not come first. I was told by the school administration: "That cannot happen," at least three times during my son's four years in high school. Guess what? After I spoke with the principal and explained my son's situation, arrangements were made to accommodate his needs.

BEING YOUR OWN ADVOCATE

During my son's junior year in high school, he was told there was no way to take the math and English classes he needed because there were not enough teachers teaching both AP classes. I was told the classes were full due to the limited AP classes. My son tried to fix this situation on his own, but he was told no.

Instead of letting it go, we went in as a team and spoke to his high school counselor. We were told there were no options to take the classes he needed. My son was frustrated and started talking to other students in his situation. It turned out that there were four students affected by the lack of class availability. I called the mother of one of those students, and we made an appointment together with the high school principal. We told her of our children's situation, and instead of telling us no, she listened to our suggestion. We suggested that she allow our children to attend AP 12th-grade English during their junior year and AP 11th-grade English during their senior year. The classes had nothing to do with each other regarding learning the subject, and although it had never been done, the Principal approved the change. Both children were able to get into all the classes they needed to be competitive for the colleges they wanted to apply to. That said, while I caution parents who hover a little too close to their students, knowing when and how to step in for your child's education is helpful.

We did not go into this meeting demanding that the changes be made; we simply stated our case and gave our suggestions. I would have preferred that my son handle this himself, but it was more than he was prepared to handle. The bottom line is that every child is different and has unique needs.

If there is a plan in place, your child will receive the education they need to be successful. I believe that a successful education is a common desire for you, for your child, and for the higher education institutes, too. Working the plan together will get your child the education they want and need. This teamwork will also set them up for success in their college application.

Do you have a plan in place? Can you answer all the questions in this chapter? If not, do not worry! By reading this book, you receive a free 30-minute consultation where you can get your questions answered! Go to www.collegereadyplan.info.

Chapter 2

What Is Most Important to Your Family – Academic Fit, Social Fit, Talent Fit, or Financial Fit (Do You Want or Need Scholarships)

Family Alignment

What is most important to your family?

1 = Most important to
8 = Least important
(rank all 1 to 8)

	PARENTS RANKING	CHILD'S RANKING
ACADEMIC FIT		
SOCIAL FIT		
FINANCIAL FIT: SCHOLARSHIPS		
ATHLETIC FIT: OR PERFORMANCE		
COLLEGE MAJOR FIT		
ACCOMMODATIONS SUPPORT		
ATTEND A TOP TIER COLLEGE		
GRADUATE IN 4 YEARS		

I meet with families every day who are trying to figure out how to get their children prepared for college. Very few think past college, and as a mother of three young adults, it concerns me. Last week, I was on a call with a high school junior and her parents. When I asked the family what matters most to them, the parents said academic fit, financial fit, and then social fit. The daughter said social fit and academic fit, but she was not concerned with the financial fit because her parents were going to pay whatever college costs. The mother quickly said, "We are not sending you to college to have fun! You need to get serious and figure out how to get scholarships because we cannot afford the colleges you are considering. I then asked the student what her dream college was. She smiled and said, "UC Santa Barbara." I got excited for her and asked her why she chose that school. She asked me if I had seen the view from their dorms! I said yes, my husband attended there, and they have a great view. I then asked her again why her dream school was UC Santa Barbara; she replied, "I just told you about the view from the dorm." She was completely serious; the view was the reason she wanted to attend UCSB. I asked her what she wanted to learn about in college or a potential major. Her father spoke up, saying she does not know her major or have a college list. A similar conversation happens at least 50% of the time I meet with families. Some students assume their family will pay for college just to find out in a meeting with me that they cannot afford it. It really makes me sad when a student thinks they will receive a full Athletic scholarship, but when I ask about their stats, I realize there is very little chance they will make a college team.

What is most important to your family: the academic fit, social fit, financial fit, or talent fit? Have you discussed this with your child? Do you all agree on what is the most important to your family? If it is the academic fit, does your child want to fight for every A at an Ivy or top-tier college? Or do they want to graduate in the top 5% of their college class so they can get into a good medical school or law school?

If it is the social fit, does your child know what they need to fit in or make friends at a college? Are they looking for a big football school or a small private school?

What about the financial fit? Does your child understand how much a college education will cost and what options are available to pay back any loans? Do they assume that you, the parents, will pay the full amount, and you were hoping your child would get scholarships or take out loans by themselves? Many families do not realize a teenager cannot take out a college loan without a cosigner. If your child gets into a college that your family cannot afford, they cannot take out a large loan to pay for college. You must repay the loan even if the child drops out of college. There is no way to file bankruptcy to remove the loan. It is with your family until you pay it off.

At this point, you may be wondering when you should have this discussion with your child or thinking *I do not want my child to worry about how we will pay for it.* Unfortunately, I've seen the downside of not discussing this before picking the colleges your child will apply to. Why would you want your child to apply to a college your family cannot afford? Many families tell me they will figure it out IF their child gets into that school. Several have told me they will use their retirement if they must, or they are just praying they will get scholarships. This lack of planning is going to cost you financially and your child emotionally if they are accepted into a college they cannot afford to attend. Having a PLAN and discussing with your children how your family will approach this will save you time, money, and heartache.

Then, some families do not want a plan to discuss college. They think it is time for their 17-year-old to adult and figure this out on their own. Would you allow your 17-year-old to buy you a home without being involved? What about a car? College is one of the top five expenses a person will encounter in their lifetime. Are you willing to take this risk? Many adults do not know how to navigate the college admission process; how will your teenager?

I spent 30 hours a week on top of my full-time career helping my oldest navigate the college admissions process. We built 33 spreadsheets and discussed the plan every day. It was not easy, so I went back to college and received my professional certification from UCSD. Even with my certification, I had to tour hundreds of colleges to find the best-fit university for my children. It was not always a fun process, and there were some tears when we had some tough discussions, but, in the end, it was critical for my children's success. Without a discussion and a plan, you can expect a lot of frustration, overwhelm, tears, anger, procrastination, lack of effort, and student loans. I do not want any family to experience that when you can avoid it.

One final thought… finding scholarships is like having a part-time job. Students spend 20 hours a week applying for independent scholarships if they want to be successful. Students can start applying for scholarships in middle school and continue applying all through high school and college. It does take effort and a plan to be successful, but so does everything else in this process. I have seen students build a calendar where they map days and times just to apply for scholarships. If you need help finding the best scholarships, book a complimentary strategy call to see which ones are the best fit for your family.

Chapter 3

If You Are Planning for a Top Tier Education, You Must Start Planning Now

It is very important to discuss as a family which college or university is the best fit for your child. Will it be a great academic fit, social fit, and financial fit? I have helped hundreds of students get into the Ivys, and when it is a good fit, it is life changing. Remember, finding a college where your child will excel, receive an outstanding education, make great connections, and graduate with little or no debt are all important factors to consider when choosing a school.

The next thing to consider is whether your child can graduate at the top of their college class to get accepted into medical school, law school, MBA, etc. It is important to have the whole PLAN before you even apply to any college. There is a perfect college for every student, and every year, I am reminded how amazing your children are. Well done, parents!

"Would You Like to Know the 'Best' Ivy League School?"

The average national rankings are also provided in parentheses

	Location (City/State)	Setting	Undergraduate Enrollment	Endowment Size	Forbes Ranking*	Niche Ranking	U.S. News Ranking	Wall Street Journal Ranking
Princeton	Princeton, NJ	Suburban	5,548	$36 Billion	1 (1)	3 (5)	1 (1)	2 (4)
Yale	New Haven, CT	Urban	6,590	$41.4 Billion	2 (2)	1 (1)	3 (5)	3 (7)
Harvard	Cambridge, MA	Urban	7,240	$50.9 Billion	5 (9)	2 (4)	2 (3) (tie)	1 (3)
Penn	Philadelphia, PA	Urban	10,412	$20.7 Billion	4 (8)	5 (7)	4 (6)	4 (10)
Brown	Providence, RI	Urban	7,125	$6.5 Billion	7 (15)	7 (10)	5 (9) (tie)	7 (26)
Dartmouth	Hanover, NH	Rural	4,170	$8.1 Billion	8 (16)	6 (8)	8 (18)(tie)	8 (49)
Columbia	New York, NY	Urban	9,739	$13.28 Billion	3 (6)	4 (7)	6 (12)(tie)	5 (11)
Cornell	Ithaca, NY	Rural	15,699	$9.8 Billion	6 (12)	8 (22)	7 (12)(tie)	6 (13)

Note: As of publishing, the 2023 rankings for Forbes were the most current.

Before you apply "early action" or "early decision" (which means applying to a college or university with an earlier deadline with different rules and acceptance rates), make sure you have a strategy. Do what is best for your child; do not just do it because of what you read online. Here is an example published by Dartmouth.edu.[3] Dartmouth announced a record-low 17% early decision acceptance rate, a significant drop from even ten years ago when Dartmouth accepted 28% of early decision applications. That year, for the class of 2018, Dartmouth had less than half the number of early decision applications than they did this year for the class of 2028. Applying early used to be unique; now, it should be used as a strategy and is not a good plan for every child.

Prospective students must understand that while Ivy League schools are highly selective, this doesn't necessarily mean they are unreachable. Students should apply strategically, considering early action or early decision options, particularly if they strongly prefer a specific school. Also, remember that the pool of early applicants often includes a higher caliber of students, which may skew the perceived benefits of applying early.

Buyer (you) beware of Early Decision; it is binding with many rules and can be very costly to a family. If you are looking for scholarships or to do financial negotiations, Early Decision is not a good plan for your family.

The overall picture remains clear: gaining admission to an Ivy League school is incredibly challenging. This underscores the importance of maintaining a well-rounded list of reach, target, and safety schools. Students should approach the application process with realistic expectations, recognizing that even with stellar grades and test scores, the odds can vary widely.

---

[3] https://www.thedartmouth.com/article/2023/12/dartmouth-offers-early-decision-admission-to-606-students-at-record-low-17-acceptance-rate

In crafting your child's college application strategy, consider not only their academic credentials but also the broader context of each Ivy League school's current admission landscape. This approach will ensure your child is well-prepared to navigate the complexities of the highly competitive college admissions process.

Not every child will get into an Ivy school or do well in an Ivy. Knowing your child and how they handle stress is very important. During my son's first week at Harvard as a Freshman, he called me to let me know he would happily accept his first B! Apparently, the English professor in a class with only 12 students shared on the first day that only one student would receive an A. My son knew he did not want to work as hard as the other students, and he wanted to balance academics and sports while still having time to join a Final Club. Knowing your child is the key to helping them find the perfect fit.

Once you decide your student is a great fit for the Ivy's, it is time to create a standout strategy and position them for success. Every student applying will have an outstanding GPA, test scores, Leadership, Community Service, impressive curriculars, and stellar letters of recommendation. What will set your child apart? Why will the admission committee pick your child over their competition?

The essays are critical to help your child stand out! What will they write about? Remember, the essays will tell the reader who your child is, what is important to them, and why they would be a good candidate for that school. Do not underestimate the essay or have someone else write it for your child. Stay away from AI, and make sure your child has their essay professionally edited by a college application reviewer.

L = Learn:
Learn What Your Child Is Passionate About

Chapter 4

Learn How Passion With a Purpose is Not the Same as Community Service

Many students are looking just to check boxes in hopes of getting accepted to college. They sign up and show up! They have no connection to the project, but it seems an easy way to accumulate community service hours. Many times, their parent signed them up and drove them to serve. Or your child decides to serve with a friend. All community service is good, but not all service is great for your child or their college applications. If your child is just putting in their time, how will they write a meaningful essay about their experience? What will colleges learn about them? Is it even time well spent with their busy schedule? Community service is usually the barrier when families meet with me to learn how to create a standout strategy or discuss positioning. The student is not passionate about what they are doing, and they do not even understand their purpose! They feel disconnected, and it feels like a waste of time. More than just checking the community service box is required if your child wants to choose their college.

Doing community service with a passion and a purpose can be life changing. Students who really understand this are the most successful in applying to college.

This is one of my favorite aspects of my career because I get to inspire teenagers to learn about themselves and their world. With electronics taking up such a big part of a child's life, I get to help them see the fun in learning who they are, what they have done to explore their passions, what matters the most to them, how others see them, and what do they want to see changed in the world. This may not sound fun to you, but this is why

I love my job more and more every day. The more teens compare themselves to their friends on social media, the more they lose confidence in themselves and their future. They compare themselves to a perfect social media world that does not really exist. As adults, we can even get caught up in it when comparing our children to others.

One of the best gifts you can give your child is introspection. Help them to see what you see in them. Share the topics you brag about to their grandparents. When you see them being a good friend, acknowledge them. When they lead another child or show compassion, tell them how amazing they are. Maybe your child acts like they do not want to hear it or that you are embarrassing them. Do not let that stop you; just be considerate and only do it when you are alone with them.

It goes without saying that comparing can lead to dangerous behaviors, but it is important to encourage them to walk beside and support each other. If you skip this step, you will find that your child has no idea what they want to achieve now or in the future. They may avoid the college planning subject altogether because they either do not think you will approve of their hopes and dreams or think that the hope may be a little too big. If you do not have this discussion with your child, they may not have the words to explain that they are good at everything and cannot choose what they want. They may have tried something in the past and were not good at it, so they quit trying. Maybe you have a child who is good at everything and cannot decide what they want for their future.

There is hope, and I want to share what we have found to be the most successful ways to help your child learn what colleges want to know. The first thing we do when a family signs up to receive support from us is to conduct several teenage diagnostic tests. These are different from the ones adults use. Once we receive the scores, we sit down with the student and help them understand what the scores mean for them now and in the future. After a full review, we then help the student verbalize what is most important to them. Is it money, status, academic challenge, teaching, doing something different every day, creating, leading, researching, building, working as a team, or working alone (to name just a few)? Because we are only there to help them and do not judge their answers, they tell us everything. We play a fun "Millionaire game" to see if they understand financial literacy (only 10% do). Then, we can show them the career they are best aligned with, the daily activities someone in that career does, and the education needed, and determine whether a robot will be doing that job in five years!

The final step is to discuss how all this information impacts the decisions they will make about their future. Do they need to attend college, and if so, for how many years? Do they want to attend college in the USA or abroad? Will they need additional college degrees, or are they better suited to learning a trade and taking some business classes? This is what a plan can do. I will provide a road map for their future and beyond. Imagine what it would have been like if you were given this opportunity when you were a teenager. Would you be doing the same career you chose? The reason why so many college students change their major at least three times while in college[4] is because high schools are not doing this work. If your child does not want to do it with you, where are they going to learn all this information?

Now, my favorite part of this plan.... In 2011, I created a Passion with Purpose plan for my son. He was too busy to do community service, and I was concerned he was choosing a career in which he would serve others for the rest of his life. I could not imagine why he did not want to do community service and yet was determined to be a doctor! So, after much

---

[4] https://nces.ed.gov/

discussion, he agreed to give me two weeks over the summer going into his senior year to help him solidify his desire to be a doctor.

That summer changed his life forever, and I have continued the same plan for all the students in the College Ready plan. If your child cannot decide how they will show colleges what matters to them and how they are going to change things for the better, please call us; we want to help you and your child. This is important when picking their college major and career. Do not leave it to chance.

If you are unsure what your child is passionate about, do not beat yourself up. Many teenagers have no idea what they are passionate about until we teach them how to figure it out. They may feel frustrated that they have no idea what they want to do after high school, but once we help them find their passion and their purpose, they get laser focused. If you miss this opportunity, your child may feel unmotivated or lost as to what needs to happen next. They may feel ashamed that they do not know what they are passionate about or have no idea what they want to do after high school or college. It does not have to be difficult, and it can be a lot of fun. We can show you how. To view our free resources that can help you, visit www.collegereadyplan.com/quickplan.

We are so committed to Passion with a Purpose and see the benefit of every teenager having the opportunity to help change the world that we have started a nonprofit where teenagers from all over the world come together and utilize their passions and advocacy. This project allows them to test their leadership skills, learn how to work in groups, and understand diversity and inclusion. They are winning International and National awards and are literally changing the world. If you think this would be a great opportunity for your child and would like to check it out, go to www.empowereducation.world. Your teenager is welcome to join and learn by participating with change-makers all over the world.

Chapter 5

Learn How to Help Your Child Stand Out and How to Position Them for Success: The Top 3 Things Colleges Are Looking For

The world is changing at a rapid pace, and so are the criteria for college admission. Here are the top three things colleges are looking for right now.

1. GPA

Your child's GPA is one of the most important factors in getting into their dream college. Most colleges consider weighted and unweighted GPAs during the admissions process, but how they use each can vary depending on the institution's specific admissions policies.

Unweighted GPA:

> **Definition:** The unweighted GPA is calculated on a standard 4.0 scale, where all classes are counted equally, regardless of their difficulty. An "A" in an honors or AP class is weighted the same as an "A" in a regular class.
>
> **Why Colleges Consider It:** The unweighted GPA provides a straightforward measure of a student's overall academic performance without considering the rigor of their coursework. It allows colleges to see how well students are doing across the board, regardless of the difficulty level of their classes.

Weighted GPA:

Definition: The weighted GPA gives additional points for more challenging courses, such as honors, AP, IB, or dual enrollment classes. For example, an "A" in an AP class might be worth 5.0 instead of 4.0.

Why Colleges Consider It: The weighted GPA reflects not only a student's grades but also the rigor of their coursework. Colleges use the weighted GPA to assess how students challenge themselves academically. A higher weighted GPA indicates that a student has taken more difficult courses and succeeded in them.

How Colleges Use These GPAs:

Holistic Review: Many colleges use a holistic review process, where both the weighted and unweighted GPAs are considered alongside other factors like SAT/ACT scores, extracurricular activities, essays, and letters of recommendation. They may look at the unweighted GPA to gauge overall performance and the weighted GPA to understand the level of challenge a student has undertaken.

Recalculation: Some colleges recalculate applicants' GPAs according to their own scale or system. For instance, they might strip out non-core classes (like physical education or arts) or standardize all GPAs to an unweighted scale to compare students more equitably.

Contextual Evaluation: Colleges often review GPAs within the context of the high school's offerings. They consider how many advanced courses are available and how a student has performed relative to what's offered. This is why some colleges request a school profile from high schools, which provides context about the school's grading policies and course rigor.

While there isn't a universal standard for whether colleges primarily look at weighted or unweighted GPAs, most schools consider both. The unweighted GPA shows a student's raw academic performance, while the weighted GPA provides insight into how much the student has challenged themselves. Students should aim to excel in rigorous coursework while maintaining strong overall grades, as both aspects are important in the college admissions process.

2. RIGOR

Is rigor important? In other words, should your student take Honors, College Prep, Advanced Placement, International Baccalaureate, or Dual Enrollment classes and get Bs, or should they take a regular schedule and get all As? I wish the answer was that simple. It all depends on whether your child would like to attend the local state college or an Ivy League university.

What does your child want to major in during college? What are your child's strengths and opportunity subjects? This is where planning is critical. Knowing what kind of college your child would like to attend before planning their classes will save time, money, and a lot of frustration.

Many times, students come to me in their junior year and tell me that they would like to attend an Ivy League school, but they have not taken any challenging classes. The reality is that, most likely, an Ivy League school will not be a good fit. The more difficult a college is to get into, the more rigorous classes a student must take while earning the best grades possible. It would not be a good fit to send a student who has never taken an AP, IB, or college-level class to a top 10 college. Academic life would be difficult, and the student would likely feel that they did not fit in. The same would be true if you sent a student who took all AP or IB classes in high school and attended a community college. The fit must be right for a student to thrive in college and to graduate in four years. Planning is the key to how much rigor, how many challenging classes a student should take, and when they should take them.

A Quick Note on Rigorous Courses

You may be wondering what AP, IB, or Dual Enrollment means and whether they are important. AP Stands for Advanced Placement. The definition of an AP class is "A program in the United States and Canada created by the College Board which offers college-level curricula and examinations to high school students. American colleges and universities may grant placement and course credit to students who obtain high scores on the examinations."

After completing an AP class, your child can take an AP exam. If they score a 3 or better on this test, many things can happen:

1. The teacher may give the student an A in the class for fully understanding the subject.

2. The student may not have to take this class in college. Depending on the college they attend, the AP exam may take the place of the college class. This option will save time and money by not having to take an extra college class.

3. If the student is an AP Scholar, which means "A high school student who has demonstrated exemplary college-level achievement on AP Exams. The student must score a 3 or higher on three or more AP Exams. The AP Scholar with Honor is granted to students who receive an average score of at least 3.25 on all AP Exams taken, and scores of 3 or higher on four or more of these exams." What does this mean to your child? Merit scholarships often come from this prestigious award.

See the AP award levels below:

AP Award Levels: IB stands for International Baccalaureate. The definition of the IB program is: "The program encourages both personal and academic achievement. It aims to challenge students to excel in their studies and their personal development. This program offers four highly respected educational programs that develop the intellectual, personal, emotional, and social skills needed to live, learn, and work in a fast-changing world. **The Diploma Program (DP)** curriculum is made up of six subject groups and the DP core, comprising theory of knowledge (TOK), creativity, activity, service (CAS), and the extended essay. Through the DP core, students reflect on the nature of knowledge, complete independent research, and undertake a project that often involves community service." Not all schools offer the IB program, so if your student is interested, they may need to transfer to another school that has been IB-authorized.

Dual enrollment: This coursework is less common than the AP and IB programs because not all high schools offer this program. The definition of the Dual enrollment (DE) programs states that they "Allow students to be enrolled in two separate, academically related institutions. Generally, it refers to high school students taking college or university courses."

Dual enrollment can benefit students by allowing them to get a head start on their college careers. In some cases, the student may even be able to attain an Associate of Arts or equivalent degree shortly before or after their high school graduation. Furthermore, participation in dual enrollment may ease the transition from high school to college by giving students a sense of what college academics are like. In addition, dual enrollment may be a cost-effective way for students to get college credits because courses are often paid for by and taken through the local high school.

Who should take these types of classes, and why are they important? First, NOT all students should take AP, IB, or Dual enrollment. This is not because a student is not smart but because these classes move at a rapid pace and teach at a college level of thinking. This may overwhelm some students with varied learning styles, which could cause their grades in other classes to suffer. Knowing the type of learner your child will be is a critical part of the college planning process. Seek advice from your child's previous teachers. Examine past grades in the subject and review test scores to understand what is best for your child. Seeking the help of a guidance counselor or Independent College Consultant may help guide you to the best path of coursework for your student. Assess your child with the survey below. See if you learn something new that will help as you plan together.

DOES YOUR CHILD KNOW WHAT THEY WANT FOR THEIR FUTURE?

Here are some questions that will open up conversations:

- DO YOU ENJOY LEARNING?
- DO YOU ENJOY BEING IN THE SAME CLASSES WITH OTHER HARD-WORKING STUDENTS?
- CAN YOU KEEP UP WITH A FAST-PACED LEARNING ENVIRONMENT?
- WHAT MAKES YOU THINK YOU HAVE TEST ANXIETY?
- IS IT EASY FOR YOU TO GET STRAIGHT A'S IN ALL EASY CLASSES?
- WHICH IS YOUR FAVORITE SUBJECT? WHY?
- HOW DO YOU FEEL WHEN YOU GET AN "A" VS. "B"?
- HAVE YOU ASKED YOUR TEACHER FROM LAST YEAR IF THEY THINK YOU WOULD DO WELL IN THE MORE ADVANCED CLASS?
- HAVE YOU REVIEWED THE CLASS BOOK OR CLASS NOTES TO SEE IF YOU ARE READY FOR A MORE ADVANCED CLASS NEXT YEAR?
- WHAT IS YOUR MAIN MOTIVATION FOR WANTING TO TAKE ON MORE CHALLENGING CLASSES?

Standardized Test Scores

Standardized Test Scores are important, especially if you would like scholarships. Parents and children find that standardized testing can be stressful and overwhelming. The two main tests that colleges consider are the ACT and the SAT. You may wonder if one is better than the other.

Both tests are equal in the eyes of college admission. In the past, the East Coast schools favored the ACT, and the West Coast favored the SAT; now, most colleges will accept scores from both. You may be wondering about the PSAT or PLAN. Both of those tests are "pre-tests" to the SAT and ACT. Should your child take both? Yes. If your school offers both, you should have your child take both pre-tests. The pre-tests are great indicators of how your child will score on the SAT and ACT.

Bonus for my readers:

Have your child take the PSAT in their freshman, sophomore, and junior years. Why? Most high schools will not inform your child that they can take the pre-tests during their freshman and sophomore years. This lack of knowledge will put your child at a disadvantage. My students with a testing plan know when to take each test and why they are taking it in the recommended order.

Standardized testing is unlike any other test your student has taken. The first time they take the PSAT is intimidating, like removing the training wheels on a bike. They may wobble a little bit but eventually find a good balance. The pressure students feel when they first take a standardized test can be overwhelming and humbling. Since the freshman and sophomore PSAT tests do not count for anything, it is the perfect opportunity for your student to practice their testing skills.

It is very important for your child to take the PSAT during their junior year. I like to call this test the "money round." Some scholarship dollars can be at stake when your student takes the junior year PSAT. The following information was taken directly from the PSAT/NMSQT Student Guide: National Merit® Scholarship Program: Students must take the PSAT/NMSQT in the specified year of their high school program. Because a student can participate (and be considered for a scholarship) in only one specific competition year, the year the student takes the PSAT/NMSQT to enter the competition is very important. Different types of scholarships will be offered, but no student can receive more than one monetary award from NMSC. National Merit® $2500 Scholarships. These awards are unique because every finalist is considered for one, and winners are named in every state. The winners are selected by a committee of college admission officers and high school counselors.

Two simple steps could mean money for college:

1. Take the PSAT/NMSQT or PSAT 10.

2. Say "yes" to Student Search Service® when you fill out your answer sheet on test day.

National Merit Scholarship Program: When you take the PSAT/NMSQT, you're automatically screened for the National Merit® Scholarship Program, an academic competition for recognition and scholarships. The PSAT 10 and PSAT 8/9 are not considered for entry. The PLAN: This is also a good practice test but is not offered at many schools, and there is no "money round." The PLAN is a good indicator of how your child may do on the ACT. The best time for your child to take this test is during sophomore year. How does your child decide which test to take? I always recommend taking the SAT and ACT at least once. Compare the child's scores, and you will have a definitive answer. After the tests, a student will receive a breakdown of their scores by category. Please review the assessment with your child.

Some questions to review after testing might include:

- Were there any surprises?

- Do the scores represent your child's strengths?

- When a college looks at your child's scores, what will they assume?

- Now comes the important question--*Did your child get the score they need to get into the college of their dreams*? That is the million-dollar question, and since every student has a different dream school, it cannot be answered in a book. It is critical to do the research and find out what past testing scores were needed to get into a particular school. An additional question to consider after testing: *If your child's score does not meet the minimum score needed for a particular school, what can your child do*? Again, planning is everything, and a test prep and testing timeline should be put together to accomplish what is needed by your child. Maybe the student gets test anxiety (which has been proven to be a real thing), or maybe the student was sick when they took the last test. It is now time to decide: does your student want to or need to take the test again, or are they willing to choose a less competitive college? If your child chooses to take the test again, you will need to decide as a family how they will achieve a better score.

- If the child did not do any test prep before taking the standardized test, they have many options to increase their score.

- Your child can go to ACT or College board websites and take the practice tests for free online.

- Your child can buy a test prep book and study from the book.

- Your child can pay to take a test prep class online.

- Your child can take a test prep class for a nominal fee at their school or library.

- Your child can pay a private test prep tutor to come into your home and work on exactly what your student needs.

- Your child can find a test prep "strategist." A good test strategist does more than tutor; they will teach the child how to beat the test. They focus on timing and strategy. Let me caution you here: *Not all test prep companies are created equal.* Educating yourself about your options will save you time, money, and a lot of frustration. College Consultants have statistics on the most successful test prep companies, and they will refer companies that have been successful for past clients. Standardized test prep for the ACT and SAT is more than just discussing the subject on the test. Your student will learn how to take tests. Students will learn how to eliminate answers quickly, find key words in a passage, and so much more. It has been my experience that test prep can make the difference in getting into a State School vs. a high-ranking university. With good preparation, many of my students have increased their SAT scores by over 300 points. One last thought on test prep: *Students can use the skills learned for the rest of their academic careers.* Every one of my college students has come back to tell me that what they learned in their test prep class helped them to be better test takers in college.

- SAT vs. ACT? I have heard parents say that a student who is good in math should take the ACT, and a student who is good in English should take the SAT. It has been my experience that these statements just are not accurate. Taking a timed practice SAT and ACT is the best way to show your child what their best test is based on the two scores. They can get rid of the lower test score and just focus on doing their best on one test. This will save you time, money, and a lot of frustration. Most colleges accept both tests. You should also know that there are "test optional colleges" that do not require applicants to take either test. Very few students get the same score on both the ACT and SAT. I have a conversion tool to assess your child's strengths on these tests. The SAT and the ACT assess different information and problem-solving skills, which is why I recommend your student take both timed practice tests at least once.

The Bottom Line

GPA is the most important factor in the college application process. If your child hopes to get into a competitive college or university, every class they take will matter. Every class they choose to take must be done in the proper order and receive the best grade possible. Taking a class that is too difficult for your child can backfire with a low grade. I recommend planning out every class for all four years to ensure that each class will get them into every college they will apply to. Lastly, standardized testing should match the GPA and rigor. If all three components do not match up on the application, colleges will question what is missing. Planning is the key to success! Every class matters, every grade matters, and every test score matters. If you are unsure whether your student's GPA and test scores match, go to www.collegereadyplan.info and set up a call so we can discuss your child's individual needs.

Chapter 6

Learn How To Evaluate The ROI of College: Can Your Family Afford College? Can Your Student Afford Not To Go To College?

The biggest question families have is: "Can our family afford college"? The answer is a resounding "YES." However, there is one caveat: Your child can afford to go to college, but only if the cost of college is planned properly. The biggest setback that can prevent anyone from obtaining a college degree is the significant financial cost of attending. While it is true that attending college may be one of the largest expenses your family will ever face, the importance of a college education has become evident in terms of earning potential within today's economy.

These questions hit home for me personally. Neither of my parents received a college degree, and I watched them work day and night to earn a good living for our family. Back in the day, it was possible to make it without a college degree if you had a lot of ambition and a strong work ethic. My mom was a hairdresser and owned several beauty salons; she made a lot of money doing what she loved to do. My dad is an entrepreneur at heart and has started and owned several businesses and real estate investments. He lives a comfortable life and enjoys his leisure time and traveling. Growing up, my dad would mention that he thought college was important for my future, but he did not tell me how to get into college. My mother thought college was not necessary, and she believed that I should get a job right out of high school like she did. My parents were loving and supportive, but I grew up unsure whether college would be the right decision for me. My parents were doing fine without the extra four years of school or debt. Because I had no idea what I wanted to do after high school, I thought I would give college a try. I am so glad that I did because what I experienced was more than just a great education!

Life lessons I learned in college

- ✓ How to live with a roommate whom I had never met.

- ✓ How to care for myself (what today's kids call "adulting"—cooking, washing clothes, cleaning, making doctor's appointments, etc.).

- ✓ I gained confidence each year that I attended college and fought for each and every one of my grades.

- ✓ If I did not go and seek a job, it would not come to me.

- ✓ Students from all over the world could be your friends.

- ✓ How to balance a budget, reconcile a bank statement, and balance life!

After changing my major five times, I learned that without proper planning, a four-year degree could take five years. (Thank goodness for summer school and winter sessions!) The reason I included this chapter is because if you, as the parent, do not see the value in a college education, your student will not either. Many parents like mine were not sure what college was all about, so they left the planning up to their children. This lack of planning and parental involvement can cost your child time and money.

Consider this: would you allow your 18-year-old to buy a home without your knowledge or input? Would you allow your 18-year-old to buy a car with a loan they had no idea how to pay back? College is an important life choice, and your child needs your help or the help of a professional. If you are hoping that your child will have a better life than you did, encourage your child to attend college. Cost should not be the main factor when trying to decide if college is worth attending. The cost of college is just one key component to consider.

8 Ways to Assure Your Child Will Receive an Affordable College Degree:

- **TAKE THE MOST CHALLENGING CLASSES**
  Strong grades = merit scholarships.

- **CREATE A STRATEGIC TESTING PLAN**
  Strong test scores = financial freedom.

- **SCORE WELL ON THE PSAT**
  A strong PSAT score can qualify a student to become a National Merit finalist, and the student will be offered many options and scholarships.

- **TAKE AP, IB, DUAL ENROLLMENT, AND COLLEGE CLASSES NOW**
  Taking these classes in high school vs. college will save you thousands of dollars.

- **CHOOSE COLLEGES YOU WILL GRADUATE IN 4 YEARS**
  Every extra year your child spends in college to finish their degree comes with a cost.

- **BUILD YOUR COLLEGE LIST STRATEGICALLY**
  In-state schools will offer different financial awards than out-of-state schools. A private school typically has more money to offer than a state school.

- **LEVERAGE YOUR FINANCIAL AWARDS**
  If your child is not offered a financial aid award, use what other colleges have offered, appeal, and negotiate.

- **PLAN YOUR COLLEGE SEARCH USING THE CORRECT RESOURCES AND TOOLS**

Remember this: What you do not know will cost you. When comparing the outcomes of attending college versus not attending college, there are several key statistics that highlight the differences in earnings, employment, and other life outcomes.

Here's a summary of some of the most significant statistics:[5]

1. Earnings Potential:

Median Annual Earnings:

- **College Graduates (bachelor's degree):** According to the U.S. Bureau of Labor Statistics (BLS), in 2023, the median annual earnings for workers with a bachelor's degree was around $67,860.

- **High School Graduates (No College):** In contrast, workers with only a high school diploma had median annual earnings of about $39,070.

Lifetime Earnings:

- According to studies by Georgetown University's Center on Education and the Workforce, college graduates with a bachelor's degree can expect to earn approximately $1.2 million more over their lifetime than those with just a high school diploma. (This information comes from a study conducted by Georgetown University's Center on Education and the Workforce)

2. Unemployment Rates:

- **College Graduates:** The unemployment rate for individuals with a bachelor's degree or higher was around 2.2% as of early 2024, according to the Bureau of Labor Statistics (BLS).

- **High School Graduates:** For those with only a high school diploma, the unemployment rate was higher, at about 5.2%.

---

[5] https://www.bls.gov/

3. Job Satisfaction and Stability:

- **Job Satisfaction:** Studies have shown that college graduates report higher levels of job satisfaction than those without a college degree. This is partly due to having more career choices and opportunities for advancement.

- **Job Stability:** College graduates are more likely to have jobs with benefits such as health insurance, retirement plans, and paid time off. They also tend to experience less job displacement during economic downturns.

4. Health and Well-being:

- **Health Insurance Coverage:** College graduates are more likely to have access to employer-provided health insurance. In 2023, about 72% of full-time workers with a bachelor's degree had employer-provided health insurance, compared to 54% of those with only a high school diploma.

- **General Health:** There is a correlation between education and health outcomes. College graduates tend to have better health and longer life expectancy, partly due to higher income and better access to healthcare.

5. Social Mobility:

- **Upward Mobility:** Higher education is associated with greater social mobility. Children born into low-income families who earn a college degree are significantly more likely to move up the income ladder compared to those who do not attend college.

6. Debt Considerations:

- **Student Loans:** One downside of attending college is the potential for student loan debt. As of 2024, the average student loan debt for bachelor's degree graduates is approximately $28,000. However, the higher earnings potential of college graduates generally offsets this debt over time. Graduating debt is the key to a winning outcome.

7. Employment in Growing Industries:

STEM Jobs: Many of the fastest-growing and highest-paying industries, such as technology, healthcare, and engineering, typically require at least a bachelor's degree. This limits opportunities in these fields for those without a college education.

While attending college has costs and challenges, including tuition and potential debt, the statistics overwhelmingly show that college graduates experience higher earnings, lower unemployment rates, better job satisfaction, and greater overall life stability than those who do not attend college. However, individual circumstances, career goals, and financial situations should always be considered when deciding to pursue higher education.

As a professional Independent College Strategist, I have turned down working with students who lack desire. If your student dislikes school, learning, teachers, time in the classroom, etc., then it's possible that your child would be better served by enrolling in a vocational school or trade school. That said, most students would benefit by attending at least some college.

I would like to share two stories about students after graduating from high school.

COLLEGE READY CASE STUDY: Affordability

Student #1: The first student I will call Mason. Mason did not like anything about high school. He thought school was a waste of time, and he just wanted to graduate so he could get a job and make money. He had been working as a busboy at a local restaurant while attending high school. He was saving to buy a new car. Mason was an average student in high school, but he knew he did not want to attend college. He loved to work on his car and enjoyed building things. Mason's parents came to me with heavy hearts, worried about their son's future. After spending an hour with Mason, it was apparent that Mason wanted nothing to do with "more school." We discussed his other options, such as attending a trade school or taking some classes at a community college. I will never forget the look on Mason's face when his father told him, "If you do not go to college, you will have to move out of our house and make it on your own!" Mason acted tough, like he did not care and would be happy to move out. Mason's mom, on the other hand, started to cry.

Student #2: The second student I will call Mila. Mila was a good student in English and History and loved taking Art classes. She was a strong student in those subjects, but she got poor grades in Math and Science. Mila had never been on a college campus, and the thought of going away to school scared her. Her parents contacted me to request that I meet with her and offer guidance. After one meeting, it became apparent that Mila knew what SHE wanted to do, but she was scared to tell her parents. Mila's dad wanted her to be practical and get a business degree. Mila's mom wanted her to follow her passion and be an artist. What both parents did not know was that Mila wanted to be a fashion designer or an interior designer. She wanted to own her own business and use her passion for art.

The smiles on her parents' faces were from ear to ear when Mila was able to explain in a college counseling session just what she wanted to do in college. Her parents were so relieved that their daughter had a passionate plan for her education and that she did want to pursue a college degree.

Case Study Fast-Forward Five Years

Mason decided he was tired of being told what to do, so he moved out of his parent's home and rented a room at a friend's house. He has a full-time job waiting tables, and he just started taking college classes. Unfortunately, all of Mason's friends have recently graduated from college and are starting their careers. They are buying new cars and have the luxury of going out to dinner and traveling. Mason now tells his story with regret and feels left behind.

Mila, on the other hand, graduated from college as a marketing major and started a job working for a clothing designer she has admired for years. She gets to employ her talents in design and set up advertising photo shoots. She lives in a nice apartment at the beach with her best friend, and she just purchased a new car. Mila enjoys her career and looks forward to designing a clothing line of her own someday.

I do not tell these stories to stereotype or speak badly of either student. I share these stories to show how each student has their own path. Even siblings will not take the same path as another family member. There is no way to predict if going to college will make one student more successful than another. What getting a college degree will do is give your student options. The more options you have in life, the better you will do! A student with a college degree will always have a degree to fall back on and use for job applications. They will not be denied a job because they did not get a college education.

I believe that knowledge is power and confidence. I have always taught my children to live life without regret. Deciding at 18 to not attend college may turn out to be a regret later. The same can be true about letting your 18-year-old take on student loans with no idea how to pay them back. High school graduation is a pivotal time! Planning will save your student from regret and debt.

The economy and its effects on education economics and recession also play an important part when planning whether to attend college. Going to college does not mean your child will not be affected by the recession, but workers with four-year college degrees earn higher wages and experience lower levels of unemployment than those with only a high school diploma.[6]

Is the cost of college worth it? FAQs

When considering whether the cost of college is worth it, I often get many questions like the following:

- My student does not know what they want to do or major in; is community college a better option? My question: A better option than what? Not going to college at all? Taking a gap year and starting college after the gap year? Staying at a community college and then transferring to a four-year college? The answer to the question is not a yes or a no. The answer is that it depends on the individual student's wants and desires. Statistically, having some college is better than none, and a four-year college degree is optimal for a favorable financial future.

- Are Ivy League schools the best option? My answer: No, Ivy League schools are not the best option for all students. If a student is

---

[6] https://www.forbes.com/advisor/education

fortunate enough to be accepted into an Ivy school, they will be competing with the best of the best. The pressure may be too much for many students, and it can also be very difficult socially. Each student must work according to his or her own plan. Success is not the name of a school; it's what the student does with an education.

- Will attending a more expensive college ensure that my student gets a better job when they graduate? The truth: There are no guarantees that any college can promise your student a better job than another college. With that said, colleges with a strong alumni network can be beneficial when looking for a job.

- What if the career my student has chosen to pursue does not provide enough earnings to cover their college debt? This is a good question, as it is always best to start with the end in mind. If your student wants to enter a career that only makes $40,000 a year, it does not make sense to get a student loan for $50,000 a year. Planning is critical here! The student should be advised to pick a college that is less expensive or one that he or she will be able to attend for free or at a reduced rate.

- You may even be asking yourself: *Why should I send my child to college if I have done fine without a college degree?* I advise you to consider your child's potential future. Opportunity is the key reason to encourage your child to attend college. Now, with more students than ever getting a college degree, it is critical to be competitive. The U.S. is no longer just a manufacturing economy. The U.S. economy is now based on knowledge and technology. The importance of a college education now can be compared to a high school education 50 years ago. College is the bridge to opportunities in the future. There are additional benefits of sending your child to college. Consider things that cannot be quantified, such as exposure to books and lectures, stimulating conversations, building relationships, and thinking outside the proverbial bubble. All these experiences allow for additional growth and development, which provides a competitive edge in the job market. Also, consider the connections your child will make with their teachers, other students, and alumni. The more connections your child has when they graduate, the more opportunities there will be for securing a great job right out of college.

Attending college provides students with the knowledge and experience they are no longer able to get from secondary education. With proper planning, your child can get a college degree without going into debt. Every piece of research I found documented the benefits of having a college degree. If the cost is no longer the reason, "why not?" I would encourage your child to at least give college a try. If you are unsure whether your child should attend college, give us a call. College Ready can help you with an assessment created for teenagers that will help you decide if college is a good match for your child.

A = Apply:
Applying to College: The Application, Leadership, Extracurriculars, Recommenders and Essays

Chapter 7

Apply a Timeline for Success: What Should You and Your Child Do, and When Should They Do It?

Proper **plan**ning is the key to ensuring your children have options when applying to college. Having a strategy and knowing when to implement each stage is critical to your child's future. Just showing up to high school and taking the classes necessary to graduate will not get a child into the college of their dreams. At best, going through high school without a plan will earn a student a diploma and possibly entrance into a local community college or state school. There are many paths that students take in high school, and no two students are the same. My desire is to give you a general guideline as to the minimum your child must do to get into a four-year college.

> **COLLEGE READY CASE STUDY: Coursework**
>
> Every class counts, and it does matter in which order your student takes each class.
>
> One of my students learned this lesson on courses the hard way. Justine and Keri were best friends and did everything together. Justine was a gifted student, and Keri was an average student. In 8th grade, the high school counselor came to their middle school to tell them what they should expect in high school. Both girls were very excited to start high school, but neither had any idea about what classes to take.

The high school counselor gave them general rules of what they must accomplish to graduate high school; however, neither of them received personal guidance. Justine had always made straight As and was invited to start high school in honors classes. Keri, on the other hand, made As and Bs but was not accepted into any honors classes. Justine felt bad for Keri, so she told her she would take regular classes so they could be in the same classes together. Keri felt much better knowing they would be together, knowing that Justine could help her if high school would prove to be too difficult. Neither girl's parents looked over their daughter's class schedules, and the girls had the freedom to choose whatever classes they wanted.

On the first day of school, Justine realized she had made a big mistake. The classes the girls chose together would be too easy and boring for her. Justine waited in line at the counselor's office to see if she could change her classes. When it was finally Justine's turn, she explained what had happened and asked the counselor if she could still be moved to the honors class she was offered at registration. He simply said "No" and told her it was too late; classes were full. Justine made the best of her freshman year and received all As. The following spring, when Justine had the opportunity to select classes for her sophomore year, she was determined to make better choices. Unfortunately, Justine was never able to get placed in the honors or AP classes because she had been put on a different track. Not only did the lack of planning hurt Justine's future, but it kept her from reaching her full academic potential.

How can you help your child plan for their Freshman Year?

In middle school, if your child has the opportunity to take a foreign language class, I suggest they take it. Also, have your child take the most challenging math they can be successful at learning. Teach your child study skills, such as where and when to study. If your child is struggling academically, hire a tutor as soon as possible. The classes your child takes in 8th grade will set the tone for their freshman year in high school. Many high schools will require that your child take a test to see if they are ready for an honors or AP class.

What to do Freshman Year

Teach your child how to prioritize.

Most students do more than just go to school. They have band practice, sports practices, community service, tutoring, and homework, just to name a few activities. Unfortunately, high schools do not teach your child how to set priorities. Each class tells your child what must be done for that class. The problem is that every teacher thinks their class is the most important. Then, in athletics, you have coaches telling students they need to practice more, condition more, and prepare to compete. The teenage to-do list is endless. Most students have no idea what to do, so they start with the easiest tasks. Usually, they do not get to the difficult subjects. If your child is lucky enough to be organized, he or she can usually get by without too much discomfort. For the other 90% of students who harbor habits like shoving homework into backpacks, losing books, not writing down assignments, and forgetting what to study to prepare for a test, there will be consequences. Problems can escalate very quickly, from small to huge. As your child transitions from the hand-holding teachers in 8th grade to the reality of high school, I suggest you spend the first few weeks helping them make a to-do list. Teach your child how to prioritize tasks because learning this very important life skill early on will head off disaster down the road.

Teach your child how to get organized.

Start with a simple backpack and binder. If your child lives on their phone, there are some great apps and calendars for time blocking. If the teachers are specific on how to set up the binders, make sure your child has set it up properly the first time. Most of the time, homework does not get turned in because the student can't find what they have completed. A supportive family can be a huge help for encouragement and accountability! The bottom line is that there are endless ways to get organized; your child just needs to find out what will work best for them. One of my students takes a photo of the classroom board at the end of every class and stores it on her cell phone to reference later.

Teach your child how to study.

If your child has always sat on the couch with the TV on and music playing, things may need to change. Establish a study desk in a quiet location with few distractions. Make sure the lighting is good and the chair is comfortable. Some students prefer to wear headphones and listen to music while they study. That is fine if they are getting their homework done and comprehending the material. It is always best to start with the most difficult tasks first so your child will feel successful and not have to dread doing the rest of their homework. Study breaks are important, and healthy snacks are always helpful. Establish a "Cell Phone Free Zone." One of my parents says that she takes her son's cell phone and iPad and puts them in a drawer until his study break. Also, remember to turn off social media notifications on the computer that your student is working on. Learning how to study now will help your child be successful in college when you are not there to help them set up parameters.

Utilize study groups.

Encourage your child to invite classmates over to study as a group. They do not need to be all straight-A students. The benefit of a study group is that each student is held accountable for doing their homework. Have each student go around the table and share their answers. If they got the answer right, have them explain it to the students who did not get it correct. For the student who got the answer wrong, have them explain where they made their mistake. This kind of discussion is beneficial for all students. It holds them accountable for getting all their work done. No one likes to let friends down!

Let them explore their passions.

Your child's freshman year should be used as a time to explore their passions. For many freshmen, it is a time to find out what they are truly good at and what they enjoy doing the most. Freshmen should try new clubs and organizations, challenge themselves with their classes, and see what they are capable of accomplishing.

Help your child set goals each semester and make them measurable.

- What grade will your child achieve in each class?

- Try out for the JV team. Audition for the school play. Don't miss a day of school. Then, at the end of the semester, revisit the goals to see how many of them your child accomplished.

- This is the first year your child should take the PSAT. Most schools will not announce that freshmen can take the test. You will have to seek out the test information, but it is worth the effort. For a quick reference, go to www.collegeboard.com for the PSAT test location options near you. Some people may question why you are having your child take the PSAT during their freshmen year. Just reply that it is a part of our college admissions strategy. If you do not want to explain the benefits of having your child take the PSAT in their Freshman, Sophomore, and Junior year, please have them call me, and I can show them the statistics on the benefits of utilizing this plan.

Have your child start his or her own community service project.

I realize this may seem overwhelming, but it is possible. Every one of my children has completed their own service project and has benefited from it personally. These kinds of projects are also good college application material.

Use the summer vacation and school year breaks wisely.

If you do not plan your child's summer, it will look something like this: Sleeping in late, going to the beach or mall, texting on the phone all day, playing video games or computer games, and following people on social media, etc. You get the picture. Most children will not ask to wake up early and have a productive summer. Again, planning is the key to a great summer for your child. You may be asking yourself, "Great, but what does that look like?" Below are some great examples of what my students have done to make the best use of their summers and breaks:

17 College Preparation Activities for Your Child to Enjoy This Summer

- INTERNSHIP OR START A BUSINESS
- RESEARCH AND GET IT PUBLISHED
- START OR JOIN COMMUNITY SERVICE PROJECTS
- TAKE A COLLEGE CLASS
- LEARN CPR OR FIRST AID
- TRY A NEW SPORT OR MUSICAL INSTRUMENT
- GO BIG WITH YOUR PASSION WITH A PURPOSE PROJECT
- VOLUNTEER IN ANOTHER COUNTRY
- BUILD YOUR LINKEDIN PROFILE
- TAKE CAREER ASSESSMENTS AND GET CLOSER TO CHOOSING A COLLEGE MAJOR AND CAREER
- WRITE A BOOK AND GET IT PUBLISHED
- LEARN HOW TO CODE
- EXPLORING VARIOUS COLLEGES THROUGH CAMPUS TOURS AND CONDUCTING RESEARCH
- EARN NATIONAL AWARDS AND LEADERSHIP CERTIFICATES
- COMPETE IN AN ART EXHIBIT
- ATTEND SUMMER ACADEMIC PROGRAMS AT COLLEGES
- LEADERSHIP CAMPS VARY IN QUALITY; SOME ARE MORE EFFECTIVE THAN OTHERS.
- WE HAVE A LIST OF OVER 100 RECOMMENDATIONS
- BONUS: APPLY TO SUMMER PROGRAMS AT LEAST 6 MONTHS BEFORE THE CAMP STARTS

We create custom opportunities for our students

I could write an entire chapter about great summertime activities. You should be aware that in addition to school year activities and academics, colleges will ask how your child spent their time while not in school. A college application will ask how many years a student participated in the activity, how many weeks a year, how many hours a week, and if they had a leadership role! There are 10-20 activities to list depending on the application. Each activity is connected to a point system, and the activity with the most points wins!

What to do Sophomore Year:

Picking the correct classes at the best times with the right teacher can be challenging, but when you have a strategic plan, it can be painless. The sophomore year is one of many changes and challenges. It is the first time that many students will take the PSAT. It is the first time your child will want to prepare for a test for which they will not get a grade. 10th grade is the year of test preparation, and the first time many students have the ability to take an AP class.

- Understanding what the PSAT is and why your child should take it may help alleviate any fears your child may be feeling. The PSAT is the practice test for the SAT test that will be used by colleges to assess your child's academic achievements. The PSAT asks questions similar to those of the SAT. The PSAT is also called the NMSQT (National Merit Scholarship Qualifying Test). I recommend reviewing any missed questions on the PSAT and learning from this test. Scoring well on the PSAT = $!

- Test preparation is not fun, and your child will not want to do it. There are many ways to prepare for the PSAT/SAT/ACT. First, you must consider your child's learning style. Do they need to see it, hear it, write it, or all three for the information to be absorbed? Plan to have your child prepare for the test using their learning style. I have found time and time again that you will get what you pay for.

- If your child is a procrastinator, although this is a difficult personality trait to change, you can show them the benefits of doing work early or at least on time. I challenge my students to prepare for a test at the last minute and be aware of their stress. Then, for the next test, I recommend having a study strategy and planned study timeline. After completing both tests, we meet to discuss what they learned. I have found that my smart, lazy students procrastinate the most. They may get through high school easily, but those habits catch up with them in college.

- Help your child find balance and manage their time. When I have students who need help in this area, I suggest they write down everything they do for a week and the amount of time they spend doing it. Next, we review the list and group the information into productive and nonproductive time. If the student is truly honest, they will see how much time they waste on social media and gaming. I suggest they approach the following week with a strategy and plan how they will use their time on a calendar "like a job that cannot be missed." The students who really want to balance their lives and stop stressing out learn quickly that time management and planning is the key to a balanced life.

- Community service should be growing and building momentum. Help your child adjust his or her mission statement and adjust expectations. Is your child still passionate about the community service they chose? How can you adjust the current project to fit their changing needs? Make suggestions on how they can grow their project. Have your child reach out to friends at other high schools and in their community so they can create a big event over summer break. Remember to keep track of all service hours and to have your child get them signed off after each project has been completed. Do not wait until they are filling out their applications to try to remember where and when they did their community service. Since College Ready is a certifying organization for two National Awards and four Leadership Certifications, all College Ready students who complete their service hours receive Gold, Silver, and Bronze national awards based on their hours completed.

- Is leadership in your student's future? If the answer is "Yes," what will that look like? If the answer is, "I am not sure," it is time to strategize how your child can add leadership to their high school experience. Will they lead in their sport, school government, music, community service, clubs, or organizations? Why is it important to start planning during their sophomore year? If you wait until their junior year, it may be too late to add the information to college applications. It is always a good idea for your student to get involved with groups that will allow them to lead in their junior and senior years. Solid leadership in well-known organizations will be important for your child's college application and help prepare your child for college and life. Leadership is important to colleges because they are looking for well-rounded leaders to make a difference at their schools. Colleges consider leaders to be mature, respected, passionate, and determined.

- Expectations and dreams should be evaluated and adjusted based on the rigor of classes and grades received in their sophomore year. It's time for a reality check to see if your child still has what it takes. Does your child still have the desire to continue with the plan to attend his or her dream college? Did your child meet the goals that were set? This is not a time to be negative, but it is a good time to check in and see if adjustments need to be made.

- Tour local colleges to compare and contrast. This is a great year to take some local college tours. Pick a geographic location where you can see multiple schools in one or two days. Visit a large public college, a small private college, a state school, and a religious school (if one is being considered). Help your child understand what it will take to get into each college. Look at the average GPA, test scores, acceptance rate, community service hours needed, cost of attendance, years to graduate, job offers at graduation, financial aid, and anything else that is important to your family.

- Does summer really matter? The answer is always going to be Yes! This summer is a great time to explore what your child may want to major in when attending college. If they want to be an architect, suggest that your child seek out adults who are doing what they would like to do after college. If your child would like to be a doctor, suggest that your child volunteer at the local hospital or an orphanage and care for children or sick patients. If your child wants to work with computers, provide the opportunity for them to learn how to write code or learn a new program. Leverage family and friends to see if your child can assist them in any way. The key is to find a summer program that will add value and help the child get closer to knowing what they want to do after college. Athletes may want to join a traveling club team or work with a coach to perfect their skills. If your child has no idea what they would like to study in college or do for a career, then I suggest they attend a leadership camp. Also, keep in mind that this summer is the best time to test prep for the SAT/ACT. Have your child sign up early for test prep support because the good ones will fill up fast.

What to do Junior Year

October is a big month for high school juniors.

- Scoring well on the PSAT will open many doors for your child. Over one million students participate in the PSAT every October. Roughly the top 50% are notified that they are Commended Scholars. Commended Scholars receive a nice letter of recognition that may be added to their college applications. The top scoring 16,000 students are announced as National Merit Semi-Finalists. These semi-finalist students will get an opportunity to apply and continue in the competition for National Merit finalists. Many colleges offer scholarships to National Merit finalists that could equal a free education.

- Your child test prepped over the summer and took the PSAT in October; now what? It is time to take the SAT/ACT. How does your child decide which test to take and when to take it? Consider when the test prep will be completed and when the testing dates will be available.

- Your child will need to decide which test is the best option to achieve the highest score. If your child needs help deciding, we have a plan that will guide you through understanding which test is the best for your child. We offer diagnostic testing with a review and recommendation on which test they should focus on. Students do not need to take both the SAT and ACT because they are considered equal at colleges and universities. After you know which test is the best for your child, we can help you understand why they missed certain questions or ran out of time. We can show you the test scores they need to get into any college or university in the world based on acceptances from the previous year. We can help you put together a test prep plan and recommend the best strategy for your child. With the correct information, your child can save time and money while only focusing on what is the best plan for your family. Beware: A test prep book is not going to get your child their best score. As a parent, I tried the test prep book with my first child, and it was a disaster. A great test strategist is different than a tutor.

The differences between a test strategist and a tutor

Test Strategist	Tutor
Focus of Process & Application	Focus on the Knowledge Gaps
"Foundational, Fundamental, CORE Skills"	Comprehensive Content Review
Detailed Pattern Analysis	General Subject Knowledge/Rules
Identifying Individual Blind Spots	Basic Time Targets
Coaching	Traditional Answer Explanations
Real-Time Self-Reflecting/Diagnosing	Vague/Miscellaneous "Silly" Mistakes
Discovering Limiting Beliefs & Behaviors	Teaching
Provide Expert Navigation	Additional Practice/Repetition
Pacing & Efficiency Evaluation	Memorizing Formulas & Rules
Streamlined Solution Strategies (S3)	Provide List of General Steps/Map

Source: Professor Mark Kover

- Teachers are important (especially the good ones). By this point, your child should have some favorite teachers. This will be very important when students choose which teachers they will ask to write their letters of recommendation. Before your child leaves for summer break, it is a good idea to ask three teachers to write their college application letters of recommendation. Be mindful of which teachers know your child the best and those who will take the time to write a great letter of recommendation. Your child will never see the letter that is written; it will go directly to the college.

- Does your child have all As? If not, then you may need to consider hiring a tutor. The honor societies at your child's high school offer free tutoring as part of their community service. If your child is too busy before or after school, you may want to consider hiring a professional tutor. Finding a great tutor could be exactly what your child needs to get an A in a tough subject. Keep in mind that the core subjects will be on the ACT/SAT tests, and your child will most likely take the subject again in college.

- Your child's junior year is the time to let their passion shine. If your child is not enjoying their extracurriculars or service projects, then they are missing out on doing things they enjoy. Writing a college application essay without passion will be a waste of time for the writer and the reader. The essay is used to add the final piece to the application puzzle. Colleges want to know who students are and what they're passionate about. There are only so many hours in the day to be productive; it is best that the time be used on something your child loves to do. Do not focus on just checking boxes to get it done; think about how the opportunity can be used in an essay or interview.

- Has your son or daughter been receiving mail and emails from potential colleges? Do all the colleges who have contacted your child really want them to attend their school? This can be an exciting time for your family, and it may be hard to decipher what is real and what is not. I will share a little secret with you – taking the PSAT/SAT/ACT triggered most, but not all, of the mail your child is receiving. Colleges send out blanket "we want you" letters to try to boost their numbers. The more applicants that apply to a college, the better it makes them look. The low acceptance rate is not a reality because most students who apply after receiving this mail blast should not be applying to that college. So, the number of applicants increases while the number of acceptances decreases, making the college look very desirable and exclusive. Be careful and only apply to colleges that make sense for your child. Before you apply, confirm it is a good academic fit, social fit, and financial fit for your child and family.

What to do during the Senior Year

- Well, you have made it! The fun is just beginning, and all your hard work will pay off very soon. Stay focused on the application deadlines and try to keep your child motivated to complete applications.

- Now, the big question comes to mind: how will you pay for college? If you have been planning academically and financially for the last four years, you should be well prepared. If you are picking up this book for the first time and your child is a senior, you may be freaking out! Paying for college is now the #1 public fear of all Americans. Unfortunately, what you do not know will cost you. Read everything you can from reputable sources, ask knowledgeable professionals a lot of questions, and hire a professional college admissions and financial strategist if you are not sure how you will pay for college. There are many myths about college funding, and buyer beware: **you do not need to pay full price.** Since I have covered this information in another chapter, I will summarize what you will want to do during this year.

Consider your options:

- Can you pay for college from your savings account without going into debt?

- Have you saved some money for college, and do you need to look at other options to fill in the financial gap?

- Are you going to make your child pay for his or her own college?

- Have you calculated your SAI (Student Aid Index)?

- Will your child receive a Merit scholarship?

- Will your child receive grants or scholarships?

- Has your child applied for local scholarships? The best scholarships often come from the parent's work or unions.

- Have you filled out the necessary paperwork to receive money from the colleges your child may be attending? Most of the free money will come from your child's college. Picking the best-fit college and having a plan will make a huge difference. The better you plan for a financial strategy, the more free money you will receive and never have to pay back.

- Communication is very important in the college application process. I suggest having an email address that is solely for the college application process. Set up an email account that is not spam-guarded, that your student will check daily, and is appropriate for college admissions. A good email address is firstnamelastname@gmail.com.

- Should your child attend college visits at their high school? Yes, if your child is considering that college, the more information they receive, the better. It is also another opportunity to ask questions and show interest in that school. If there is a sign-in sheet, make sure your child signs in. Many colleges track your child's interest in their school. They may track college tours, follow them on social media, and track time spent on their website. Some colleges do not track your interest, and I am happy to share which ones do and which ones do not.

- The time has come to pick colleges to which your child will apply. If you have no idea where to start, refer to my chapter on picking the right school. If you still have no idea where to apply, then ask your high school counselor for advice. You can also hire a professional college consultant to pick the colleges that are best suited for your student. If you are looking for merit money, I can show you the most generous colleges and how much money they gave students last year.

- Getting organized will be very beneficial during the application season. When I started College Ready, we used binders and dividers. Now, we have a custom password-protected portal for students to have up-to-date information in real-time. Be careful what you read on Google and social media—most of it is not true.

- Now it's time for your student to apply to colleges. Different applications will open on different dates. Your child will want to write down all the important dates to remember. Deadlines are just that—nothing will be accepted after the college deadlines have passed.

- Should your child apply for early decision? Early action? Priority decision? Restrictive Early action or Regular decision? If that sounds like new vocabulary or another language, you will want to get familiar with these terms. There is money involved, and you will want to know the pros and cons. Early decision admission programs allow your child to apply early, and if he or she gets in and loves it, no other applications are needed. We like to call this one and done! By applying for early decision, you are telling the college that if you are accepted, you are 100% committed to going there. When you get accepted to an early decision college, your child will be forced to withdraw applications from all other colleges. The downside is that your child will not have many financial options or the ability to negotiate.

- If you are hoping for some financial aid, your student will want to apply for early action or regular decision. Procrastination will be a huge problem for your child in this process. If students miss a deadline, they will not be able to apply to that college until the following year unless they offer open enrollment. Unlike early decision, early action allows your child to apply early to show their interest in a college, but it is not binding if they get accepted. The biggest benefit of applying for early action is that it reduces the stress of waiting for a decision. Early decision deadlines are usually in November, and regular decision deadlines are from December through January. Remember, college is a business, and if they know you are applying Early Decision, there is a slightly higher chance of acceptance. By applying Early Decision, you are telling them you will accept their admission and pay full price. If your child is qualified, they can say yes and bind you to the cost.

- What are secondary supplements, and does your child have to complete them? In addition to the Common Application, many colleges will also require their own supplement. This can be completed on the Common application site if the college participates in the Common application. Otherwise, it will have to be done on the college's individual website.

- Aren't all essays the same? The answer is no; college application essays are very different from high school English class essays. Since a high school English teacher has not been taught how a college essay reader views an essay, it would be a bad idea to have your student's English teacher proofread the college application essay. Most English teachers can check for grammar and spelling, but most are not qualified to do the editing. Colleges are looking for something totally different. It is always best to have a professional application editor proof your child's essays before they are submitted. Not all essays are created equal, and the essay could be the deal breaker. The admissions reader has minutes to read the essay, and if it does not impress them, your child's application will be put in the wrong pile.

- College application fees and what you should expect. Although applying to college is usually not as expensive as actually attending college, there are several associated fees. Most applications range from $40-$150 each and can be paid in several ways (or waived).

- If a college uses a Common Application, the fee can be paid through the Common Application website with a credit card.

- If a college does not use the Common Application, they will provide instructions on how to pay the fee.

- Fee waivers are available if your student qualifies. Check with each school for details. Fees are typically due upon submission of the application.

- Accept the financial aid offer or make an appointment to appeal it.

- Send your child's final transcript to their college.

- Complete housing and health forms.

- Start searching for that perfect roommate. Be brutally honest when answering the roommate questionnaire.

- Submit AP scores.

- Register for the Orientation program at the college your child will be attending.

- Hug your family and friends and send out thank you cards to all the supporters who helped get through the process.

- Students who are applying to a specialized program, such as art, architecture, music, dance, or theater, may be asked to submit a portfolio of work. Make sure to check with your child's college; each has different requirements. There is also an additional information section in the Common Application where your child can upload any extra information they wish to share with colleges.

- If your child makes any changes to their spring class schedule, your child will have to report the changes to all the colleges where they submitted an application.

- Community service hours should be logged in and submitted to your child's high school counselor for approval. This is a great time to finish the service project or transfer it to a younger sibling.

- Many guidance counselors may be willing to send a mid-semester update to students who wish to update their applications after the original deadline, sometime during the spring semester. This may include any awards that your child has won, accommodations given, or generally anything that might bolster an application. Remember: this is just an update, so you must have submitted the full application by the original due date first.

- A college may request additional testing or additional proof of community service or leadership. Have all the details in order before you hit send!

- What is TOEFL, and does my child need to worry about it? If your child is from a non-English speaking country or is a non-native English speaker, he or she may be required to take the TOEFL to show proficiency in English. Check with your child's colleges to determine if this is required.

- I always suggest starting with the result in mind. What do I mean? Help your child think about what they would like to do after they graduate college. Do they want to have a career in social services, law enforcement, medicine, engineering, education, etc.? What is your child's potential income going to be once they graduate college? Does it make sense to go into debt for the career they want, or would they be better off going to a less expensive college? Would it be best for your child to be at a college where they graduate at the top of their college class? These are all things to consider before applying to college. Have a plan that makes sense for your child and your family. If your child has hopes of going on to grad school, where will the money come from? Will an undergrad education set your child up for grad school acceptance? Every decision must be planned out so the student will spend the least amount of time in college and save money by knowing where the best place is to invest.

- What happens after the college acceptances arrive? Your child still needs to finish strong. Some colleges will check final grades, and they can rescind their offer. Senioritis is real, and many students struggle to stay focused after spring break. Remember: they still have AP testing or IB research and finals to accomplish. AP exams matter, and students taking an AP class should sign up to take the AP exam if it makes sense for their strategy. If your child gets a 3 or better on the AP test, they may not have to take the same class in college. This will save both time and money! Every college has its own guidelines surrounding AP scores, so you will want to check the college's policy. If you research this information before applying to college, you may be able to pick a college where your child will be able to start as a sophomore. In other words, you can save a year of tuition. This is a huge savings!

- Planning your next move will be important emotionally to your child and financially to your family. Discussing all your options with your child can be stressful but very important. I put together a spreadsheet for my students to show them their options (i.e., colleges that offer the best financial package, have programs so students can graduate in four years, offer the best deal for the money, and have a success rate with job placement).

- What if they get put on a "wait list?" This can be frustrating and have financial consequences. How will you get your child off the wait list? You will need to have a plan for this. More and more colleges are turning to the waitlist to keep good candidates until they hear a no or a yes from others. You cannot just ask to get off the waitlist; you need a plan.

- After your child has said YES and accepted a college offer, what happens next? Here are some last-minute details that will need to be done:

    o Most colleges now give your child a special website with their own mailbox. I suggest activating this email ASAP and checking it at least once a day. All communication will come through this email, including scholarship and grant information. Have a plan on who will check this email and how often. I met a family a few years ago that did not check their child's student email account and lost a $25,000 scholarship because they did not respond in time.

Grants and Scholarships by State (California)

You do not want to miss any deadlines for awards. This information is time-sensitive.

Check with your child's high school counselor regarding what the school does regarding Cal Grants. Most colleges do the work, but not all. If you are a California resident, here are the key details about Cal Grants you need to know:

1. **GPA Verification**: The California Student Aid Commission (CSAC) requires GPA verification for Cal Grant applicants. Most high schools and colleges in California automatically submit their students' verified GPAs electronically to CSAC by the required deadline.

2. **Need-Based Scholarships**: Cal Grants are indeed need-based financial aid programs for students who are residents of California attending eligible institutions, which include the University of California (UC) system, California State University (CSU) system, California Community Colleges, and qualifying independent and career colleges in California.

3. **Award Amounts**: The award amounts can vary depending on the type of Cal Grant and the educational institution. For UC colleges, the maximum award for a Cal Grant A can be up to around $12,000 to cover tuition and fees, though exact amounts may vary slightly each academic year based on state budgets and tuition rates.

For the most current information and specifics regarding eligibility, application procedures, and award amounts, it's always best to consult the California Student Aid Commission's website or the financial aid office at the UC college in question.

The system is a bit different for Home School Programs. Colleges will want to see their SAT/ACT scores. If you need help with this, please confirm you have the correct information for each type of college or university.

CONGRATULATIONS, YOU DID IT! Parents, take some time to reflect on all that your child has accomplished and celebrate with them to show your support. There are still many details that need to be completed, but you now have time to relax and enjoy. For students, it is now time to celebrate graduation from high school and dream of future plans. Wear college clothing with pride and remember how hard you worked to get what you wanted.

Chapter 8

Applying: A Standout Application

Now that you understand the importance of your child's GPA, rigor, and standardized test scores, I will share some other important topics colleges will be considering while reviewing your child's application.

Class Rank: How does your child compare to his or her classmates? The College Board defines class rank as "a mathematical summary of a student's academic record compared to those of other students in the class." Your student's ranking will show how they compare to other students in his or her high school with the same opportunities. Class ranks are determined by comparing a student's GPA to the GPA of peers in the same grade. So, if your student is a senior at a high school with 700 seniors, each of them will receive a number from 1-700. The person who has the highest GPA will be ranked #1. Your child's class rank also determines his or her class percentile. If your child's school does not list a student's percentile, colleges may ask the student to calculate it.

Here is an easy way to figure out your child's class percentile based on their class rank:

1. Divide your child's class rank by the number of students in their grade.

2. Multiply by 100.

3. Subtract that number from 100. For example, if there are 700 students in your child's grade, and he or she is ranked 105th, then your child is in the 85th percentile [because (105/800) 100=15, and 100-15=85]. Percentiles matter! Some states offer high school students guaranteed admission to state universities if they have a certain class rank.

More important class rank information to consider:

- Class rank can be weighted or unweighted.

- Class rank is only one criterion that colleges use to determine a student's academic abilities.

- Some high schools no longer use class rank due to growing concerns that it causes students to take fewer challenging courses.

- Your child's class rank can typically be found on their high school transcript or report card.

- If your child's high school doesn't include class rank, it won't negatively affect their chances of getting into college.

- A desirable class ranking can also mean FREE money!

Application essay: This can be the "deal breaker!" If your child's essays do not match his or her high-caliber GPA and test scores, the entire application will suffer.

Consider this: The application reader has several hundred applications to read. If every student has a perfect GPA and every student has a perfect SAT or ACT score, then the essay has the potential to be a powerful final decision maker. The college application essay is like nothing your child has written before. High school English focuses on the mechanics of writing, not necessarily how to write the perfect college application essay. It is important to note that not all topics are good for this essay. Your child's voice must authentically shine through, and the opening paragraph must hook the reader into continuing to read the essay.

Therefore, it is critical that three things must NOT happen when your child is writing their essay.

1. Do NOT use AI to write essays or answer questions on an application. The colleges have tools to detect the use of AI, and if they suspect it was used, the applicant will receive a no thank you.

2. Parents, Do NOT write the essay for your child (or pay a professional to do so). The application readers have seen it all, and they will be aware of unauthentic essays that are not the work of your child.

3. Do NOT be your child's essay editor. While it is difficult to back away from this step in the application process, as a parent, you are too close to the subject. You will likely not read your child's work with a critical eye. It is best to hire a professional essay editor who understands what colleges are looking for.

Remember: college admissions are very competitive, and I guarantee that your child is competing with other students who have access to everything they need to be successful. I know it is tempting to save a little money and ask your child's English teacher to edit the application, but beware: academic teachers are not always looking for the same things the colleges are looking for. A good College Consultant will offer essay editing as part of their program. It is worth its weight in gold, and it's one of the services I offer all my clients! You also want to ensure your child's essay adds to their application. Avoid having your child repeat the sports, activities, and leadership positions that take up most of their application. A "slice of life" story that captures your child's personality and core values can be valuable. Adding something interesting, like an anecdote or an activity they are especially passionate about, can help your child's college essay. These techniques can help the application reader get to know your child on a different level.

Your Common App essay is your chance to shine beyond just grades and test scores—it's where your unique story comes to life! By weaving your personal experiences into a compelling narrative, you can captivate the admissions committee and truly stand out. Storytelling allows you to showcase your authentic self, highlight your strengths, and paint a vivid picture of the value you'll bring to the college community. Remember, it's your voice and story that will leave a lasting impression!

Recommenders: Is your child well-rounded and valued by their teachers, coaches, or people in your community? Picking the best recommenders is very important to the application. Before your child jumps to ask just anybody to write a recommendation letter, consider how the recommender writes. Is the coach a great writer? Will a particular teacher be able to offer the "real you" to colleges? If your child is not sure whether to ask someone to recommend them, then that candidate is probably not the correct person. Your child's recommenders should know your child by name if they pass them in the hall. The recommender should know what kind of person your child is. Ideally, a recommender should have a story to tell about the student. The best recommenders tend to be English, Math, Science, History, or Language teachers. There is a strategy on how your child should pick the recommenders, and they will want to make sure to ask at least three teachers if they would be willing to write a letter of recommendation. This is not the time to surprise a teacher who does not know them well.

Interview: If your child gets the opportunity to be interviewed by one of his or her potential colleges, what is a good next step? If your child can speak well to teachers and adults in general, then I recommend that he or she interview with the school. Preparing for the interview must not be overlooked. What your child wears, the questions they ask, and how they represent themselves are very important. Again, colleges are looking for similarities. Does your child match his or her GPA, test scores, essay, etc.? Is there anything that stands out about your child? If your child is confident in himself or herself, this can be a huge win! The interviewer will write a report and send it back to the application reviewing team. The interview not only shows the college that your child is interested, but it also confirms that your child would be a great match for the college. I spend a whole day preparing my student to know what to expect and all the do's and don'ts in preparation for the interview. Most interviews will be conducted via Zoom, so make sure they are in a room that is clean and the lighting is bright.

Extracurricular Activities: When it comes to applying to colleges, it is no longer viable to just be an academic student. Colleges and universities are looking for well-rounded and balanced students. Going to school, studying, and gaming on the TV do not amount to an impressive college resume.

Questions to consider regarding your child's extracurriculars:

- Does your child have a theme that captures all the activities they enjoy, or are they all over the place?

- Has your child stayed with the same activities throughout middle and high school, or have they bounced around inconsistently?

- When your child is not in school, what are they doing?

- Is your child shopping, at the beach, hanging out with friends, watching TV, playing on the computer, spending time on social media and their phone? (Beware: Those activities are all red flags! Point your child in a direction with more focused passions.)

- Does your child participate in clubs, sports, or organizations?

- How much time do they spend at these events outside of school?

- Is your child using their free time to help others?

- Is your child working on being a productive citizen?

- Have they started or led a club?

Colleges want to know everything about your child, and what they do in their free time will tell schools a lot about the student/leader they are.

Important: Did you know that the Common Application asks for ten activities, honors, and awards? Did you know that the UC Application asks for 20 activities, honors, and awards? It is important that the activities are listed from most important/impressive to least impressive. Does your child have 20 activities, honors, and awards they would be proud of?

Extra-Curricular Activities Passion/Talent

Teenagers can be complex, and it is important at this time in their lives to discover and decide what they are passionate about. When it comes to college applications, it is time to ask your child: What have you done with your passion? If you asked your child to list ten things they are passionate about, and if they only had five minutes, could they do it? What would you list if I asked you to write down ten things your child is passionate about? Enjoying what your child does with his or her own free time will go a long way in helping colleges see the kind of person your child will be if accepted into their college. Colleges are looking for students with passion! They are not looking for a student to come to their college and just take away an academic education. The goal is that your child will be a dynamic and active presence on their campus, one that will lead others to be the change they wish to see in the world. Athletes and students in the band have a slight advantage with this question. In most cases, it is obvious that a student-athlete has a passion for his or her sport and that they work hard to perfect their skills. Students in music or band must practice long hours and show passion for their talent. Dedication and determination tell a lot about your child. Activities must be meaningful to them, but their passion should also be an integral part of their high school experiences. What makes your child unique? What sets your child apart from all the other candidates? How will your child be remembered? Your child will most likely have to answer questions like, "What makes you unique?" or "Tell me something that I cannot read in your application." How would your child answer this question? Do they have something about them that will make them a better candidate than other students? How will they be positioned from the other tens of thousands of students who are applying to the same school? If they begin their planning process early enough, there should be plenty of time for your child to pursue at least one meaningful activity about which he or she is passionate.

Positioning

Once you figure out how to help your child stand out, how will you position them? If their application does not make sense to the admissions reader, they will have questions. If the questions are not answered in an essay, this can cause them to be denied admission.

Diversity and Inclusion: Has your child proven they work well with others? Are they a loner, or do they have proof they value other students' opinions? Have they been successful in leading others to create positive change?

Geography: Where do you live, and why do you want to attend the college to which you are applying (especially if the school is not in your state)?

What colleges want to know from your child:

- Why our school?
- Why do you want to leave your friends and family?
- Is your child running from something or to something?
- Are you willing to pay out-of-state tuition if your child is accepted? In some cases, going across the country for college tells the application editor that your child is confident and mature.

Community Service: What has your child done for someone else that did not benefit them? Colleges want to know the answer to this question. Is your child a caring and compassionate person? A quick anecdote: While I sat down to write this chapter, I was approached by a 9-year-old who offered me some lemonade. She went on to tell me that she was collecting donations for the Make-a-Wish charity. In the process of serving me lemonade, my new friend explained why she was raising money. She told me that during her flag day at school, someone came and told her school that the Make-A-Wish foundation gives kids their last wish. She told me that all the money she had raised was going to help someone she had never met do something very special. The passion that my new friend showed at nine years old will take her far in life. The goal of a community service project should be to do something your child is passionate about. Not all community service hours are created equal. I will share with you two examples to demonstrate the difference.

COLLEGE READY CASE STUDY: Community Service

STUDENT 1: I have one student that I will call Trevor, who hired me in the fall of his Senior year in high school. He had a 4.59 GPA and solid test scores. However, he only had 20 hours of community service (which he needed to graduate from his high school). His hours came from a random assortment of projects like dog washing, car washes, collecting canned goods, etc. None of these service hours were bad, BUT they just did not show one clear picture of Trevor's passion. He would show up, do his time, and then he would just leave. For Trevor, service was more about checking off a list of hours than enjoying the act of service.

STUDENT 2: My second student, whom I will call Molly, started the College Ready Stand Out Strategy plan the summer of her 8th grade year. She was passionate about helping others; however, she could not figure out what she wanted to do for her passion with a purpose service project. Her brother had gone to Africa that summer to volunteer at an orphanage in Kenya, and his stories had touched her heart. However, for Molly, the photos of the children brought her to tears. How is it that she and her friends had everything they needed, and these children had nothing? It just did not seem right, and during one of our 1-1 meetings, we created a Mission Statement together. Who did she want to help? (The children of Africa), What did she want to do for them? (Educate the children so they can learn how to care for the next generation). Where would she focus her passion? (After a ton of research, she found the greatest need was in Uganda). When would she start and finish her passion project? (She chose to start immediately and would stay focused on this project until she started college and then would hand it off to another student with the same passion for empowering children through education.

I could write a whole book on Molly's passion project, but I will summarize it here. Molly was able to find a contact in Uganda through a family friend. They would meet weekly to build the foundation of the passion project. During these meetings, Molly would get so excited because you could see how impactful her mission would be. One year later, Molly had 49 students from all over the world who met once a week to discuss the needs of the children. In 12 months, they raised over $18,000! They built two classrooms that would educate over 300 children who otherwise had no opportunity to be educated. They lived in a rural part of Uganda with no schools or formal education. Molly earned four National Gold awards and four Leadership Certifications and was accepted into five top-tier colleges. Her essay told her story, her story helped her to stand out, and her leadership got her accepted! Not only that, but she earned over $300,000 in scholarships. That is what Passion looks like with a purpose! Molly's passion is still very much alive, and if you would like your child to join her group, go to www.empowereducation.world to learn more and get involved. (There is no cost)

This project is just an example of what our students do to help others in need. Every one of our students has a personal story of impact.

I hope you can see the difference between just checking a box and living with purpose. The essays bring it to life and help your child stand out.

Community Service Leadership: When you think of the word "Leader," what is the first thing that comes to your mind? Maybe it is structured leadership at school, like the Associated Student Body (ASB). Maybe it is the Drum Major or Conductor of the school's band. What about the captain of your child's sports team? Boy Scouts or Girl Scouts often come to mind, especially if the child has achieved the Eagle or Gold award. Some children may find their leadership in a club or service project. The list of Leadership opportunities is long and varied. Do you know what type of

Leadership is the most impressive to colleges? It is the child who rises to lead in the same organization over time. It is the child who sees a need in their community and leads others to provide help. It is a child who can lead people whether they are older, younger, or even the same age. It is one who can organize and lead a group to accomplish their goal. It is a child who may captain their soccer team to victory while teaching younger children how to follow their dreams of someday competing in their sport.

Getting accepted into college is not an easy process. With the proper plans and knowledge, it can be accomplished without losing your mind. Many parents save for college but will not hire a tutor, test prep instruction, or a college planner. I suggest getting a tutor if needed, hiring a great test prep company, and seeking the help of a knowledgeable college planner. By seeking help from experts, your child will have a much better chance of getting into the college of his or her dreams and earning merit money! When your child completes their college applications, I recommend that you or a professional review the application before they click Submit.

Navigating the Application Process

RESEARCH COLLEGES	PREPARE APPLICATION MATERIALS	COMPLETE APPLICATIONS	SUBMIT APPLICATIONS	AWAIT ADMISSION DECISIONS	EVALUATE AND ACCEPT OFFERS
Explore different colleges and universities that align with your academic interests, career goals, and personal preferences. Consider factors such as program offerings, graduation rate, alumni connections, campus culture, location, job placement and cost.	Gather all necessary documents, such as transcripts, test scores, letters of recommendation, and a personal statement and essays. Polish your application materials to showcase your strengths and unique experiences.	Carefully fill out each college application, ensuring you provide accurate and complete information. Pay attention to deadlines and follow all instructions to ensure your application is submitted successfully.	Submit your completed applications, either through the college's website, The Common Application, Coalition Application, State Application, or Private Application. Keep track of your application status and any additional requirements or follow-up needed.	Be patient and wait for the colleges to review your application. During this time, continue to maintain strong academic performance and participate in extracurricular activities. Think about what you can do now to get off the waitlist.	Once you receive admission decisions, carefully compare the offers and select the college that best fits your academic, financial, and personal needs. Consider financial negotiations, reconsiderations, and compare awards.

Chapter 9

Applying Your Plan to Crush the Interviews and Get Off The Waitlist

The excitement is building. Every day, your child is checking their email, looking for that perfect college acceptance letter. Tears of happiness and maybe a few frustrated moments are sure to find their way into your home. Each day, your child is waiting to hear back from first-choice colleges. What can your child do during this exciting yet frustrating time of waiting? I recommend using this time to go on admissions interviews, plan Spring Break college tours, continue focusing on GPA, and apply for scholarships. Some colleges will not make their decision on your child's acceptance until they have been interviewed by an admissions advisor or alumni. Your child should use this interview to his or her advantage because it is their last opportunity to shine. This interview will offer your child an opportunity for an exchange of information and represents a chance to ask well-thought-out questions and highlight your child's strengths and interest in the college.

Before the interview:

Help your child prepare by practicing interviewing with another adult.

Research the college website for information that you find interesting or impressive. These are good talking points! Write them down on a notepad and bring them up during the interview.

Most interviews are now done via a Zoom call. It is very important that you consider their surroundings, the lighting in the room, what is behind them on the wall, etc.. I also review with my students how to look and speak confidently. Your child may not be aware that they play with their hair when they are nervous or touch their face a lot. Help them with their non-verbal skills so they look confident.

Spring Break is a great time to visit/tour your child's top three colleges. Not only is it a great family bonding trip, but it is also a time for your child to have a reality check. As the school year ends, the reality of leaving for college becomes real. Some children embrace it and start to plan for what they will bring to college when they leave for school. Others become very quiet and distant. They may be having a difficult time imagining that they will not see their family members daily. Some children become terrified and start to second-guess going to college at all. One of my students asked me who would make them food and do their laundry. Most children are a little fearful of the unknown. By going to the potential colleges with your child, you can address all their concerns so that your child can make the best decision for him or herself. Some children cannot wait to live in a new state, while others are very content to continue to live at home. Most colleges will have sent out their acceptances by Spring Break, but not all of them. Try not to jump to conclusions or make assumptions. Some colleges just take longer than others.

College tours: What is important to look for at this point in the decision process? If your child has only taken a virtual tour of their top schools because they were too far away or because it is cost-prohibitive for them, this tour will be critical. If you have been on all the campuses before, then you will want to look for certain things about the campus that may concern you, such as safety.

Recognizing and fighting senioritis

How to help your child finish strong! Senioritis: noun. A crippling disease that strikes high school seniors. Symptoms include laziness and excessive wearing of comfortable clothes, old athletic shirts, sweatpants, athletic shorts, and sweatshirts. Also, features a lack of studying, repeated absences, and a generally dismissive attitude. The only known cure is a phenomenon known as GRADUATION!

Did you know that colleges could rescind offers to students if their grades decline or if they are found doing inappropriate things on social media? It does not happen often, but there is a chance. I would never wish that problem on any student. Senioritis is real and seems to get worse after Spring Break. It is always best to have an open discussion with your child about what can potentially happen if he or she makes poor choices.

Every year, colleges rescind offers of admission, put students on academic probation, or alter financial aid packages because of some effects of "senioritis." Colleges have the right to deny admission to an accepted applicant if a student's grades drop during senior year, and many schools state this information directly on the letter of acceptance. Admission officials can ask a student to explain a drop in their grades and can revoke an offer of admission if they feel it is warranted. Colleges do not receive final grades until June or July, so students may not learn of a revoked admission until July or August, after they've given up spots at other colleges and have few options.

What colleges expect from your child their Senior year:

Colleges see both a mid-year grade report and a final (year-end) transcript. They expect students to maintain previous levels of academic success. If your child always receives As and Bs, then a C or D may be a problem.

Colleges expect seniors to complete courses that they are enrolled in, including high-level courses. If your student lists classes on a college application and then decides to drop or change their classes, they must share the new class schedule with the colleges they applied to.

How to keep your Senior on track:

Keep your child excited about going to college. Communicate openly about what can happen if they get lazy or lose focus.

Have your child maintain a challenging course load. If they have always taken AP, IB, or Honors classes and they decide to take early release or basket weaving, they are sending the wrong message to colleges.

Also, encourage your child to enjoy the last year of school. Suggest that they attend football games, go to the prom, attend graduation festivities, and participate in clubs, sports, and volunteer work.

If your child needs something new and challenging, encourage them to commit to an internship or career-focused job. This will help them in the future to make sure they are majoring in a subject that they will love to call a career.

Keep a calendar of your child's activities and deadlines. Help them to stay focused and prioritize what is most important. Focus on things like AP tests, college applications, senior-year events, and extracurriculars.

Avoid constant nagging about applications and the application process. Try to keep a balance in your home of work and pleasure. All work and no play will cause your senior to shut down. Keeping your child focused will not only protect them against senioritis but will also leave them in a stronger position to transition from high school to college.

N = Negotiate: College is a Business —Do Not Pay Full Price

Chapter 10

Valuable Lessons and How to Negotiate: What You Don't Know is Costing You (SAI/FAFSA/CSS)

Did you know that you do not have to pay full price for college? Few things are more depressing than researching your child's first choice college to find out that the cost of attendance is out of reach. The sticker price can be shocking, and it has brought many parents to tears. Paying for college has just emerged as one of "America's Top Fears." This chapter will help to put your mind at ease. The only families that pay "full price" for college naively do not know any better.

Let me ask you a question: Would you allow your 17 or 18-year-old to buy a car without being involved in the process? Or even crazier: Would you allow them to purchase a new home without your advice? One year of college can be the equivalent of buying a new car! Your child's four-year degree can be equivalent to purchasing a new home. If your child picks the wrong college or the wrong major, the cost can be equivalent to that of a new home and a new car. The cost of attending college gets more expensive every year. According to recent data, college costs have continued to rise dramatically over the past few decades. From 1995 to 2024, tuition and fees have surged significantly:[7]

---

[7] https://nces.ed.gov/

- **Private Universities:** The average tuition and fees at private national universities increased by 179%.

- **Public Universities (Out-of-State):** Out-of-state tuition and fees at public universities rose by 226%.

- **Public Universities (In-State):** In-state tuition and fees at public national universities saw the highest increase, soaring by 296% since 1995[8]

Student Loan Debt Statistics

The rise in tuition has led many students to rely heavily on loans, with the total student loan debt in the United States reaching approximately **$1.76 trillion** as of late 2023. This includes $1.60 trillion in federal loans and about $130 billion in private loans. On average, students are graduating with **$37,056** in student loan debt, and nearly 7% of all loans are currently in default.[9]

Financing Options

Families often face difficult choices when it comes to paying for college. Some common options include:

1. **Borrowing:** Many students and parents take on substantial debt, contributing to the growing student loan crisis.

2. **Tapping Into Savings:** Families may use retirement funds or home equity, which can compromise long-term financial security.

---

[8] https://www.investopedia.com/student-loan-debt-2019-statistics-and-outlook-4772007

[9] https://thecollegeinvestor.com/student-loan-debt-statistics/

3. **Negotiating**: Many families do not realize that college is a business. Why would you not negotiate with a business to get the best deal?

However, about two-thirds of students attending public or private colleges do not pay the full price, thanks to federal and state grants, scholarships, and institutional awards. Schools most likely to provide significant financial aid tend to be liberal arts colleges, baccalaureate colleges, and master's-level universities. In contrast, research universities are typically less generous with merit-based scholarships.[10]

Understanding all available financial options, including grants, scholarships, and strategic school choices, is crucial in managing the rising cost of higher education. If you're navigating the complexities of college funding, exploring these alternatives can help you make informed decisions and potentially reduce the financial burden on your family. Planning and understanding your options are more critical than ever in this rapidly changing environment.

When it comes to paying for your child's higher education, **Planning** is your best option. Planning is the key to finding the perfect college, picking the correct major, and graduating debt-free in four years with a job waiting for your child. Yes, all this is possible. And I have many happy parents and students who can prove it! Let me share the stories of two of my students.

---

[10] https://www.studentloanplanner.com/student-loan-debt-statistics-average-student-loan-debt/

COLLEGE READY CASE STUDY: Planning to Pay

The first student, I will call Steven, and the second student, I will call Annie. (Names have been changed for privacy reasons). Steven was raised by a loving, middle-class family in California. Neither parent attended college, and the thought of sending a son to college scared them to the point that they never discussed the subject in their home. That said, Steven was on his own to figure out his future. He was a star soccer athlete in high school and on a club soccer team. His dream was to get an athletic scholarship and go to any college that would allow him to play his sport and go to college for free. His parents had managed to put away $32,000 for his college education in a 529 plan, which could only be used for college fees. In the first semester of Steven's high school senior year, he was injured just before his athletic season started. He would not be able to play high school or club sports. He was not too concerned because he already had two verbal commitments from colleges. However, as the semester progressed, Steven became depressed. He was not able to play the sport he loved, and he was not motivated to go to school. His grades were so bad that he almost didn't graduate from high school. The two verbal promises never came to fruition. Steven's future did not look good. He pulled away from all his friends who were excited about attending college and started hanging out with a tough crowd. His parents did not know what to do to help Steven, so they went to his high school counselor for advice. They were told it was "too late for Steven to apply to any colleges" and that "he would have to go to community college and apply next year." In turn, Steven's parents were upset that they let their son down by failing to plan.

Annie, on the other hand, had a different experience. She had two parents who both worked very hard to provide for their family. One parent had attended college, and the other had retired from the military. Annie was self-motivated and driven to succeed. Her dream was to become an Emergency Room Doctor. Since Annie's parents were busy with their careers, they knew they did not have the time to help Annie with her college plans. They hired an Independent College Consultant, who Annie started working with in the summer of her 8th grade year. Her College Consultant helped her map out every class she would take—from her freshman year to her senior year in high school. They put together a test prep plan with a timeline of each test and when she would take them. They came up with a community service project Annie was passionate about and could lead. They discussed clubs and organizations and how to balance everything she wanted to do. They even considered how they would leverage her sport to complete the college plan. Annie had a plan starting with her first class in high school. She followed the plan that was created for her strengths and opportunities. She took each test in the proper sequence and timing. Her service project impacted so many lives that it was featured in a local newspaper. Annie applied to fourteen colleges that were perfectly selected for her and her dream of becoming a doctor. She was accepted into eleven colleges, five of which offered her a FULL ride (tuition-free) education! Annie was now in charge of her future and could choose which college she would call her home for the next four years. Her parents used the money they had saved for her undergrad tuition to pay for her medical school. Annie had no debt after she graduated from college and medical school.

You may be in disbelief, but both stories are 100% true. There are hundreds of examples of planning (or a lack thereof) just like these. Having a plan for your child's academics, testing, community service, leadership, letters of recommendation, athletics, essays, and family finances will allow your family the same opportunity Annie had. Just as no two students are the same, no two families are the same. You do not have to lose your mind and your bank account while going through the college planning process.

Keep reading as I will show you why you do NOT need to pay full price for college. There are ways to earn a wonderful college degree without paying sticker price or going into debt. At this point, you may be asking yourself: *How do I find the best college deals?*

PLAN TO DECREASE THE COST OF COLLEGE

1. Maintain a Strong GPA.

A strong GPA (your child's weighted grades 10-11th grade) is the best way to get into college and attend for free. Many colleges all over the country offer a free education to attract valedictorians, top 10 percent graduates, and students who have demonstrated strong leadership skills. Every school is looking for the best students. In the college world, reputation is everything. Schools are looking to graduate the best and brightest students to attract the next generation.

2. Test scores can get your child a free college education.

If you score well on your PSAT, you may become a Merit finalist (Scholar, Finalist, or Semifinalist). Achieving the best scores on the PSAT will open many doors. Colleges—both private and public—will contact you, offering tuition, room and board, etc. This is one of my favorite options to share with my students. I believe it empowers them to think big and to know that if they work hard to succeed on these tests, they can earn a free college education.

3. Take dual enrollment or AP classes.

By taking dual enrollment classes while still in high school, your child can save on the cost of a college class. In a lot of cases, students can enter college at a sophomore level and save a year of tuition expenses. Taking the AP tests with a score of 3 or better will give your child the opportunity to skip several basic college classes. By choosing either option, you will save both time and money. For more information on dual enrollment, you can find what you need from the National Center for Education Statistics at https://nces.ed.gov/.

4. Look for colleges with strong merit scholarships.

Many colleges offer large merit scholarships to attract great students. These can range from a few thousand dollars up to full tuition, room, and board. Getting a merit scholarship is not easy. Most schools will have you compete for them by writing an essay or going through an interview process. Private colleges typically offer larger merit scholarships because they can. Most private universities have a strong alumni association that donates millions of dollars to help the college attract strong students. It is also important to consider less selective schools because they tend to offer better merit scholarships to appeal to the top students. If your child has a high GPA and test scores, there is no reason they cannot get a reduced or even free education. Remember, GPA and test scores are not enough. Colleges are looking for the full package. Having a plan and negotiating with a university is the key to your child's success. Even state schools can be expensive. Also, it's important to consider the entire package—the cost of attendance, years to graduate, alumni connections, and the success rate of getting a job out of college.

5. Choose a college your child will graduate from in four years.

Many American college students do not graduate on time. Not graduating in four years will cost your child an opportunity cost. Buying a car, home, getting married, having a family, etc. Every additional year it takes your child to graduate from a public four-year college will cost an average of $22,826 (report by Complete College America). It is important for your family to know the graduation rate for all the colleges being considered before making the decision to submit an application. Look for private colleges that have a proven track record of getting their students out in four years. If you plan properly in high school, your child can graduate from college in three years. There are classes that your child can take in high school that will earn college credits. There are also accelerated college programs with majors that will allow your child to graduate in three years.

6. Look for out-of-state public colleges or international schools with special pricing for out-of-state students.

Many out-of-state schools offer "special pricing" for out-of-state students. They will either offer you the cost of tuition equal to an in-state student or reduce costs to attract students with diverse backgrounds. Several out-of-state colleges offer merit scholarships for out-of-state students based on their GPA and test scores. If your child is willing to go to college out-of-state, there are many schools that will offer them outstanding scholarships. Think outside the box! You may also want to consider international schools like Oxford, Cambridge, or KTH Royal Institute of Technology, where you can get a free technological education. My stepdaughter chose to attend college in Prague (AAU). She was able to get a dual US and European business degree in three years for $27,000 total!

7. Look for private schools that meet 100% of your needs.

Do not ever let your financial needs keep your child from attending college. Since every family has a different financial situation, this can be challenging to understand. I will try to simplify this for you.

DISCOVERING YOUR STUDENT AID INDEX—A FINANCIAL AID TOOL

You have two options.

Option One: Schedule a complimentary consultation at www.collegereadyplan.info, and we can calculate your SAI for you.

Option Two: Visit the website of a college your child would like to attend. Find the financial aid section of the website and search for the SAI (Student Aid Index) calculator. Enter the required information and press enter. The calculator will provide you with your family's Expected amount of money that you will be asked to pay for that college. If your SAI is $15,000, you will be expected to pay that college $15,000. If the tuition is $30,000, you will have to pay $15,000 (your expected contribution), and you will have to figure out how you will pay for the rest. Many private colleges have a generous alumni group and strong financial backing. Often, they will offer to pay 100% of what you cannot pay over your SAI. So, if your SAI is 0, you can go to many colleges for FREE! There are more of these colleges than you are probably aware of, and they do not advertise their giving. Knowing the most generous colleges and how to position your child to get accepted will save you thousands of dollars.

As of 2024, numerous colleges continue to commit to meeting 100% of demonstrated financial need for full-time, degree-seeking undergraduates. Currently, around 75 colleges meet this criterion, including well-known institutions like Harvard, Princeton, Yale, and Stanford, among others.

This means that if a student is admitted and their family cannot cover the full cost of attendance, these schools will provide financial aid packages that fill the gap between what the family can afford and the total cost, often without requiring loans.

These schools use information from financial aid applications like the FAFSA and CSS profile to calculate a student's demonstrated need. If you can prove financial need, these colleges will cover what you cannot afford, making them an excellent option for students from lower-income families who qualify academically.

Working with a knowledgeable College Consultant can help identify these schools and guide you through the process of lowering your Student Aid Index (SAI), ensuring you maximize your chances of receiving generous financial aid packages. Effective planning and understanding how to present your financial situation can significantly impact the amount of aid you receive, making it entirely possible—and legal—to reduce your SAI and make college more affordable. Then, you negotiate!

8. Look for four-year colleges that your child may commute to so you will not have to pay for housing and meals.

The cost of living at college is expensive, and it's not usually rolled into the cost of attending. Living on campus can range from $8,000 to $15,000 per year. Look for colleges you can drive to and plan your schedule to attend classes only a few days a week. Another money-saving option is to take online classes. This will not give you the "full college experience," but if money is what is keeping you from going to college, it is another option to consider.

9. Take advantage of local community colleges for summer school and winter break.

When your child is home for the winter break or summer, consider having them sign up to take a class or two at a local community college. This will allow your child to take some basic classes at a reduced price. It could also empower your child to graduate on time or early. This is a great plan to save time and money. But keep in mind that community colleges are overcrowded. You must register as soon as the courses are released.

Current statistics on community college graduation and transfer rates:[11]

1. **Community College Transfer Rates:** Recent data indicates that only about 33% of community college students transfer to a four-year institution, and fewer than half (48%) of those students earn a bachelor's degree within six years of starting at a community college. This means that only about 16% of all community college students ultimately earn a bachelor's degree after transferring to a four-year institution.

2. **Graduation Rates for Community College Students:** According to the latest report, only 18% of students who start at community colleges and transfer to a four-year institution complete their bachelor's degree within two years of transferring. This highlights the challenges community college students face in achieving their educational goals within the expected timeframe.

---

[11] https://ccrc.tc.columbia.edu/press-releases/new-reports-all-backgrounds-transfer.html

These statistics underline the importance of effective transfer pathways and targeted support for community college students to help them successfully complete their degrees.

10. Work while attending college or join the military.

Several colleges provide opportunities for you to work while attending college in exchange for free tuition. You may also want to consider committing to one of the nation's military academies or military colleges, where you can attend college for free. Planning and research are critical to this process. In this case, not knowing where to find the best deals on college will cost you! Looking at your planning options earlier in the process will help steer your child away from overpriced colleges so that he or she may focus on strong colleges where they will receive a free or reduced fee.

Be Your Own Advocate For Financial Planning

Our Nation is functioning under a $1 trillion debt crisis! This is out of control, and you do not want your child to become a statistic. For the first time ever, the national student loan default rate exceeds the credit card delinquency rate. Also, note that student loans are one of the few types of debt that cannot be discharged with bankruptcy! If you plan properly and negotiate with the colleges and universities, you will NOT need to get a student loan, and you will NOT need to go into debt! It is important that you are careful whom you listen to. Not everyone has all the facts and the correct information. One step you can take is to hire a College Consultant who can help you avoid the national crisis that comprises the staggering cost of college. Don't become a statistic!

Before your child applies to any college, I highly suggest you discuss the following topics as a family:

1. Assess family finances.

College is a huge investment in time and resources. Openly discuss what money has been saved for college, how much you as parents are willing to pay, the possibility of loans and debt, and which colleges are a good fit financially. If you are not comfortable discussing this with your child, you need to decide what you are willing to do to support them. I have met many parents who worry that their child is only going to college to get out of the house and party. I have the perfect suggestion for these parents! Discuss your concerns with your students and offer to make them a deal. If they pick a college that does not make sense financially, you can either tell them No or offer to meet them halfway. Some of my clients have made a deal that the student may attend the college of their choice and take out a loan to pay for it. If the student graduates with a certain GPA determined by the parent, the parent will pay off the student loan. This is obviously a judgment call by the parent.

2. Decide whether the child's desired college is a want or a need.

Why does the child want to attend a certain college? Is it because their boyfriend or their best friend is going to attend there? Is it because they have a great football team or a Greek system? Try to get your child to verbalize why they want to attend a certain college. Write a list of pros and cons! Then, ask them if their choice makes sense financially compared to all their other options. Is it worth starting their adult life with debt?

3. Determine if the major they pick will pay for their wants and needs after they graduate.

Picking the wrong major can be costly. On average, most students change their major three times while attending college. If not done properly or with a plan, these changes can cost you both time and money. Before your child picks a major, ask them to write down ten things they are passionate about. Set that list of passions aside for the time being. But do follow up by asking your child what they would like to major in and why. If your child is unsure and has little or no direction, consider that a red flag! I recommend working with your child to figure out their passion or seeking the advice of a professional.

We start our students with self-analysis, skills assessments, and core values. I could not find a good tool for high school students to use, so I created one for my College Ready students. It is not helpful and is very frustrating for your child not to know what they want to do in the future. The quicker you can help them find the best-fit opportunities, the easier the next several years will be for your family.

Remember, not every college has every major. Picking a college based on a *maybe I want to do something* attitude is asking for trouble. Ask your child to pick three majors and make sure each college they apply to offers at least two of their options. Changing majors while in school may mean taking unnecessary classes, which means wasted money.

This comprehensive list of college majors is designed to help parents guide their teenagers in exploring various fields of study.

Major	Description
Accounting	The study of financial transactions, financial reporting, and auditing.
Aerospace Engineering	Focuses on the design and development of aircraft and spacecraft.
Agriculture	Covers farming, crop production, and resource management.
Anthropology	The study of human societies, cultures, and their development.

Major	Description
Architecture	The art and science of designing buildings and structures.
Art History	Examines historical and cultural developments through art.
Biochemistry	Explores chemical processes within living organisms.
Biology	The study of life and living organisms.
Business Administration	Focuses on managing and operating businesses effectively.
Chemical Engineering	Involves the design of processes for producing chemicals.
Chemistry	The study of matter, its properties, and reactions.
Civil Engineering	Deals with designing and constructing infrastructure projects.
Communication Studies	Explores human communication and media.
Computer Science	The study of computers, algorithms, and programming.
Criminal Justice	Focuses on the legal system, law enforcement, and corrections.
Economics	The study of production, consumption, and transfer of wealth.
Education	Prepares students to become teachers and educators.
Electrical Engineering	Involves the study of electrical systems and circuits.
English Literature	Focuses on analyzing and interpreting literary works.
Environmental Science	Addresses issues related to the environment and sustainability.
Finance	Covers investment, capital management, and financial markets.
Geography	The Study of Earth's Landscapes, Environments, and Places.
Geology	The study of earth's physical structure and processes.

Major	Description
History	Explores past events and their impact on present and future.
Hospitality Management	Focuses on the management of hotels, resorts, and tourism.
Human Resource Management	Covers recruitment, training, and employee relations.
Information Technology	The use of technology to manage and process information.
International Relations	The study of global politics and international affairs.
Journalism	Focuses on gathering, assessing, and presenting news.
Law	Prepares students for careers in the legal profession.
Marketing	Covers advertising, sales strategies, and consumer behavior.
Mathematics	The study of numbers, quantities, and shapes.
Mechanical Engineering	Involves the design and manufacturing of machinery.
Medicine	Prepares students to become doctors and medical professionals.
Music	Focuses on music theory, performance, and history.
Nursing	Prepares students for careers in healthcare and patient care.
Philosophy	Explores fundamental questions about existence and ethics.
Physics	The study of matter, energy, and the universe.
Political Science	Examines government systems and political behavior.
Psychology	The study of the mind and human behavior.
Public Health	Focuses on improving community health and preventing diseases.
Sociology	The study of society, social behaviors, and institutions.
Theater Arts	Covers acting, directing, and stage production.

Major	Description
Urban Planning	Focuses on the development and design of urban areas.
Veterinary Medicine	Prepares students for animal healthcare careers.
Women's Studies	Examines women's roles, contributions, and issues.

Again, a plan is very important.

Finally, based on their specific major, there are plenty of follow-up questions to consider:

- What does your child want to do after graduation?

- What are your child's career goals and aspirations?

Starting with the end in mind will save your child a ton of time and money. If your child picks a career that you know will never allow them to earn enough to be able to pay back their college debt, consider this another Red Flag! It is time to start from the beginning and discuss the cost of living on their own and taking care of their family. Try not to shoot down their dreams while still being realistic about their future.

4. Note the graduation rate of the colleges your child is considering.

Less than 1/3 of all public and non-profit four-year colleges have a 4-year graduation rate of 50% or better. What does this mean to your child? Each additional year will cost more money. Not only will the additional year be an added expense, but it will also take money away from your child. No salary for an additional year, no retirement for an additional year, no health insurance for an additional year. A low graduation rate usually means that the college is overcrowded, and students cannot get the classes they need to fulfill their requirements.

5. Learn about the acceptance rates at the colleges your child would like to apply to.

Acceptance rates show supply and demand for a specific school. A school with a low acceptance rate means that it is in high demand and will most likely not be offering many merit scholarships.

6. Consider the size of the college.

Approximately three-quarters of all colleges have less than 5,000 undergraduates. Most students prefer colleges with more than 5,000 students. There are many more smaller schools than there are large schools. Because the larger schools are better known, they do not have to offer money to compete. You are more likely to get a better financial package at a small school.

7. Know that other add-ons to college add up.

Beyond tuition and room and board, please consider these expenses when completing your budget: Health insurance, gym fees, parking and car registration, activity fees, dorm damage deposit, computer insurance, dorm room stuff, technology fees, lab fees, Greek life, spending money, travel money, and the cost to buy or rent books.

When you buy a house, you hire experts like a realtor, bankers, brokers, escrow agents, etc. When you pay taxes, you hire a bookkeeper and a professional accountant. Trying to navigate this college process alone can make you crazy. The reality is that even with all the information you can find online, you do not know what is reliable. You do not have an expert offering you suggestions on what you can do to NOT go into debt. This process can be scary and overwhelming for your family. But knowledge equals stress relief and savings.

There is so much to know about the college application process, and what you do not know will cost you and your child both time and money. If you would like to save yourself a lot of time and frustration, go to www.collegereadyplan.info for a complimentary Zoom call to get your questions answered.

Chapter 11

Negotiate to Get Big Scholarships – Build a Strategic List of Generous Colleges

Question: Do you know how much it will cost you if you pick the wrong college? Answer: I have seen a college transfer cost a family up to $1,000,000! (time, money, and energy).

Deciding which college is the best for your child:

As a parent, this can be one of the most frustrating stages of the college planning process. When you ask your child, "What is your dream school?" or "Where do you want to go to college?"—the answer will often be, "I don't know!" This is not uncommon. Your child is most likely a little nervous about picking the wrong school. So, how do you help your child pick the college that is the best fit for them? Each college and university is just as unique as your child. So, your child should pick a college based on his or her personal and career interests, career goals, past academic success, and test scores.

Parents often want to know where and how they can get assistance for the daunting task of finding the right school.

Below are some options for you and your student:

- Meet with your student's high school counselor. Be careful; they have no idea how much your family can afford or how you will plan to pay for college.

- Buy a book about college selection and hope it is up to date.

- Attend college open houses.

- Research colleges on the Internet. I spent 30 hours a week with my first child.

- Contact each college and speak with the admissions department.

- Ask a neighbor or friend with experience to help you. Be careful; their child may love essays, and yours may not. Everyone will have a unique experience.

- Hire a professional to guide you. If you need help getting your child into their best-fit school, hire an Independent College Consultant. If you are looking to help your child, get into the school of their dreams and out debt-free, hire a College Strategist (this is what I do). If you need help figuring out how you will pay the gap after scholarships, hire a Financial Planner or Insurance Agent. Make sure it's someone who specializes in finding the perfect College Match but also understands the return on investment. Remember, college is a business, and they are looking at their bottom line while also trying to find the best student to be successful at their institution.

What you do not want:

Let your child pick a college based on its identity as a top-ranked college. Caution! Colleges can inflate their rankings.

Consider this: if a college sends out letters of interest to thousands of underqualified students who then apply to that college that they are NOT fit for, the acceptance rate for that college is inflated. The lower the acceptance rates, the higher that college is ranked. You may be feeling frustrated that you are not sure what information you can trust online or which college rankings are legit.

Buyer beware: College is a money-making business, and many schools will do everything they can to persuade your student to apply to their college. Do not believe everything you read. It is important to know the graduation rate for a student to graduate in four years at each college your student is considering. Research the value of the degree and major your student is considering. Know what internships and job opportunities are available upon graduation. Ask what financial aid is awarded and to what percentage of students.

When I help my students start the college matching process, I consider the following four criteria:

1. I assure all my students that there is a perfect college for them. They may not even know the name of the school yet. There are perfect matches for 5.0 students as well as 3.0 students; they just need to know where to find these schools.

2. I assure all my students that the college picking process does not need to be stressful. So much stress comes from the fear of the unknown and from misinformation they receive from friends. Knowledge is power.

3. I help my students change their focus from "The best college" to the "Perfect College" for that student. From size to geographic location to campus culture to academic caliber, colleges can vary as widely as the students applying to them!

4. I explain that they need to follow a sequence of steps to achieve success. I always start with the end in mind. For many students,

choosing a college is their first major decision. Going through this process will provide lifelong skills such as taking initiative, making decisions, showing tenacity, and being responsible. With guidance, this process can be exciting and enjoyable. The result can be powerful: graduating from college in four years and having a job waiting for the student after graduation.

For Parents: Try to remember that you had your chance at a college choice. This time around, it is your child's turn to pick the college that he or she wants. You can assist your child by encouraging him or her to go step-by-step through the process. Help your child take the planning process seriously. Encourage them to think, reflect, research, and choose carefully. Remind your child that the process will take time; it cannot be accomplished in a day. I recommend setting aside an hour a week to discuss the process and how they are feeling and progressing. Throughout the process, try to encourage and support your child's research skills. Ask open-ended questions that can't be answered with a short yes or no. Set your expectations upfront with timing and next steps. All the while, keep in mind that your child's GPA must come first. Without a solid GPA, there would not be a need for a college search.

For Students: You have worked very hard to be able to decide which college to choose. Do not rush through the process; instead, take your time. Know that you will be living at your college for at least four years. Consider the location, the size of the school, and all the elements that are important to you.

This process can be intimidating. There are no rights or wrongs, just choices to make. If this process seems overwhelming, I recommend that you seek help from an experienced college strategist.

Be careful not to listen solely to friends or well-meaning adults. College is a choice, and big decisions can be difficult for a teenager or young adult. Picking a college is an important choice that will lead to success in the future. If your child invests time and energy into the college search, they will find many colleges in which to choose from. If your child chooses not to seek information but takes the "wait and see approach" to college selection, they will most likely be disappointed with their final college options. Your child's first decision is whether they have a desire to attend college. If the answer is YES, then I suggest the child make a list of the outcomes they desire from a college education. Simply stated, the child needs to write down or verbalize exactly why they want to go to college. If your child is still not sure, you can count on him or her not following the steps to find the best-fit college. Your child's second decision should be when to start school. Does your child want to take a gap year or jump right in after high school? The gap year has become an increasingly popular option for a student who needs a break or wants to travel before pursuing further education.

What about taking a Gap year?

Taking a gap year between high school and college can offer students a wealth of personal and educational benefits, but it also comes with certain drawbacks to consider. Following are some key pros and cons of taking a gap year.

Pros

1. Personal Development

A gap year can provide time for personal growth and self-discovery. Students can explore their interests more deeply, which might help them choose a major or career path.

It offers a break from the academic pressure of school, allowing students to recharge and gain a fresh perspective before entering college.

2. Real-World Experience

Traveling, volunteering, or working during a gap year can offer practical experiences that build life skills such as independence, time management, and problem-solving.

Engaging in different cultures and communities can broaden one's worldview and enhance social skills.

3. Enhanced College Performance

Students who take a gap year often enter college feeling more focused and motivated. They may have a clearer idea of what they want to achieve academically.

4. Opportunities for Internships and Work

A gap year can be a good time to gain work experience, intern in fields of interest, or build a resume, which can be beneficial for future job searches.

Cons

1. Cost

Depending on the activities planned, a gap year can be expensive. Traveling, volunteering abroad, or participating in structured gap year programs can require significant financial investment.

If you do not have a plan for your gap year, it will look like a long vacation to a college and your future job opportunities.

2. Loss of Academic Momentum

Some students may find it challenging to return to a structured academic environment after a year off.

There's a risk of losing the routine of studying and academic rigor, which might make the transition to college more difficult.

3. Peer Progression

Watching peers move on to college can create a feeling of being left behind, which can be emotionally challenging for some.

It might affect social relationships as friends disperse to different colleges and new environments.

4. Admission and Scholarship Implications

Some colleges and scholarships might require additional documentation or reassurances that the gap year was spent productively.

There may be limitations or additional steps required to defer admission or scholarships.

Conclusion

Consider your personal goals, financial situation, and educational plans before deciding to take a gap year. If used effectively, a gap year can provide valuable experiences that enrich a student's life and enhance their academic and career paths. However, it's crucial to plan the gap year thoughtfully to ensure it serves its intended purpose of growth and development. Do not go into a gap year, thinking it will be easier to apply to colleges. Based on what I have seen, it proves to be much more difficult. Also, be very careful and understand the rules of a gap year. At most colleges, if you take any college classes, you will have to apply as a transfer student and wait until your child has 60 transferrable units.

Choosing the perfect college for your child

Choosing a college should not be a stressful or traumatic event. Your child may look at this process as positive and exciting or negative and overwhelming. The better they are informed about choices, the less stressful this process will be.

If your child follows these simple steps, he or she will feel more in control of the situation.

1. Analyze themselves as a student.

2. Review the qualities that will make a college right for them.

3. Use all the resources listed above to select the colleges to which they will apply.

4. After receiving all their acceptances, your child will get to pick which college is the best fit. Misinformation can lead to a bad college match.

Once the final three colleges have been determined, it is time to start the negotiation process!

Following is a list of common misperceptions to consider when selecting a college.

Misperception	Truth
A good college is difficult to get into.	There are thousands of great colleges for every kind of student.
The kids that get into the best schools have some secret skill that my student does not have.	Every child has individual gifts and talents; try not to compare your child to peers.
If your child has no idea what to be when he or she grows up, your child is not ready for college.	At least half of my students had no idea what they wanted to do after college until we started working together. It is normal for high school students not to know what they want to do. Do not let that hold them back from applying to college.
If your child does not get into college X, you have failed as a parent.	This is not true! The brand name of a college does not equal success or failure.
Picking a college because it is on some "best list" in a magazine is NOT a good strategy.	A good strategy is doing your own research or seeking out the help of a professional (an expert) that will help guide you to the best fit for your child.
There is a perfect college for every student.	Believing that there is only one perfect college for your child is setting your family up for a lot of heartache. If planned properly, there will be several perfect match colleges to choose from.
Good schools cost a lot of money.	You do not need to pay more money to get a better education. If your child's best match college costs less than other colleges, you should be celebrating.

Misperception	Truth
The cost of a college should be the main quality to consider.	There are ten colleges that offer free tuition in trade for working at the school. A four-year degree from one of these colleges will not cost anything. Knowledge is the key to success.
A child must fit in a perfect student mold to be accepted.	Colleges consider many things when deciding who to admit to their college. They look at course selection, grades, test scores, extracurricular activities, where the student went to high school, athletics, etc. Colleges must pick a diverse class of students. If they have too many business students, they will have to let other teachers go.
Be careful not to fall into the trap, "EVERYONE thinks that college X is the best" so that is where I want my child to attend.	With the right preparation, your child will find a school that is just the right fit!

Important considerations before accepting a college offers

1. Is the college being considered a reach, comfort, or safety college for your child?

2. Based on past acceptance stats, what are your child's chances of being accepted?

3. If your child is accepted, can you afford the college fees?

4. If you pick a college because they have your major, and then your child changes his or her major, will your child still feel as though the college is a perfect match?

5. If your child got into the college, would he or she really want to live there?

6. Will your child be happy at a religious college or at a school without religion?

7. If your child is an athlete, does he or she want to play in college at a D1, D2, D3, or a club team?

8. If your child gets accepted as a Scholar Athlete, will he or she get to live with non-athletes? Some athletes will not get to pick a major; the coach will choose the major for them. Will your athlete get to play or ride the bench?

9. If your child is a Merit Scholar, would she or he be happier being a big fish in a small school or a small fish in a big school?

10. What is the reality that your child will stick with their chosen major all four years?

Chapter 12

Finances: College Without Student Loans – Negotiate

Is it possible to attend college and graduate without a student loan? Yes. I have helped many students navigate the financial process. With a strategic plan, it is possible. Below are two students who have recently graduated from college and their financial success stories.

> **COLLEGE READY CASE STUDY: Finances**
>
> Kathy came to me as a freshman. She had big dreams but little money. I helped her formulate a plan to leverage the PSAT and increase her GPA. After working together for four years, Kathy was accepted into 11 colleges and chose Harvard. Harvard met 100% of Kathy's financial needs. Working hard and having a plan made Kathy's dream of going to Harvard a reality!
>
> Susan came to me as a junior with a dream of becoming a professional photographer. Her desire was to attend Chapman University in California. Financially speaking, her parents could afford Chapman, but Susan did not want to burden her parents. We worked together to create a portfolio to win her a full scholarship to Chapman. Susan's parents could not be happier with the result. They used some of Susan's college savings and took a nice long vacation after Susan left for college. They also bought a new car with the money saved in just the first year.

I share these student success stories to show what great planning can do for a student. There are many more client stories just like these happy endings to a long journey. Planning is the key to not having to take out a student loan. What you do not know will cost you!

Common Mistakes Families Make When Saving for College:

Waiting Too Long to Start Saving

Some families consider college costs after it is too late. The best time to start planning for college is when your children are toddlers. The FAFSA looks at the second semester of their sophomore in high school and the first semester of their junior year.

Putting Money into the Wrong Savings Accounts

Not all savings accounts will protect you from college tuition. Working with a College Strategist or College Financial Planner is the best way to learn where your money is safe. If you read the FAFSA (I have several times), they tell you where to put your money and where colleges will look for their share. You can choose where you want to save your money and maybe get a 1-2% return, or you could hire a financial advisor who specializes in college financial planning. A specialist like this would advise you that there are many options available. Knowing your options and having time to implement the best strategy is how you send your student to college without a student loan.

No Saving Plan

You plan to face the reality of college when your child gets there. This strategy could benefit you if you are a "need-based" family. If you have nothing to offer colleges, and your child is a strong academic student, colleges may meet 100% of their need. This becomes a huge problem, however, if your child is an average student. Colleges do not pay for average students; therefore, your child may not receive any money from the college and will have to depend on government aid and student loans.

We Don't Need to Save...We Have Plenty of Money to Pay for College

You might have the funds today; however, it's smart to have a backup plan in case your financial situation changes. If you have extra money to invest at the end of the year, there are safe places to secure your money for your child. There are also places to save your money that will hurt your child's chances of getting scholarships and grants. Working with a professional who knows all the unique strategies that are safe for you and your child is very important for the future. An advisor who only offers you a 529 plan is NOT a College Funding Specialist!

Not Taking the PSAT Their Junior Year

If your child chooses not to take the PSAT, they are choosing not to get a free or reduced education.

Not Taking AP Exams

If your child chooses not to take the AP exams, they are choosing to give up the chance for a free year of college. If your child takes enough AP exams and scores a 3 or better on the AP exams, there are many colleges that will let your child enter as a sophomore. This means you will save one year of college tuition.

Not Taking Any College or Dual-Enrollment Classes In High School

If your child chooses not to take the most challenging classes available to them, they are choosing to give up potential money from colleges. Some of my students take online college classes while they are in high school or during the summer months. Getting good grades in these classes gives them a huge advantage. Colleges like to see students with rigor. If your child demonstrates that he or she can handle the tough classes, colleges will want them. If colleges want them, they will offer them money to attend!

Unfortunately, there are many ways to make financial mistakes, and most of the time, it's because families simply do not know any better. As mentioned earlier, you have options. Hiring a professional who can help explain your options will save you both time and money.

Understanding financial aid and student loans is not easy, but it is beneficial. There is a lot of small print, and the buyer must beware. Do not sign anything without thoroughly understanding the terms and conditions. Please do not assume anything when it comes to college finances. Many middle-class families assume they will not get any scholarships or aid. That is simply not true. I have helped many middle-class families get huge scholarships.

Financial Award Letters

Financial award letters will look different for all colleges. Below are the common elements you will want to compare:

Merit Aid/Scholarships: Colleges award merit aid to deserving students using individual college guidelines. This aid is in the form of college-based grants and scholarships. Some scholarships have criteria such as a specific GPA, enrollment requirement, or certain income requirements. Make sure to ask if the scholarship will be good for all four years or whether your child will have to reapply every year. Scholarships help students pay for their own education and do not have to be paid back. Scholarships are available to students who demonstrate achievement in academics, athletics, the arts, or community service. Scholarships may be awarded by the college or by other organizations.

Work Study: If you qualify for financial aid, colleges will award you work study. This is money your child will earn at a job, usually on campus, while in college. This money can help to offset college expenses.

Federal and State Grants: These awards do not need to be repaid. Some grants are based on a student's GPA.

Student Loans: Colleges offer subsidized and unsubsidized student loans.

A subsidized loan can be a good investment. The government pays the interest on the loan while the student is in college. They offer low interest rates, and multiple loans may be consolidated into a single payment.

An unsubsidized loan has low interest rates, and multiple loans can be consolidated into one payment. The recipient may opt to pay interest while enrolled, or you can allow interest to accumulate while enrolled and during the 6-month grace period.

Parent Loans: Although some colleges add these to the award letter, these loans should not be considered part of the aid package. If they are included, subtract them from the overall total. With a parent "Plus" loan, parents can borrow up to the total cost of an education, minus any other aid the student receives. Plus loans have a variable interest rate. Be very careful with these loans!

What is the best way to compare awards? You can create a spreadsheet and compare each college.

Comparisons to consider:

Estimated Cost of Attendance

- Tuition and fees
- Housing and meals
- Books and supplies
- Transportation
- Other costs?

Grants and Scholarships your student will receive

- Grants and scholarships from the college directly
- Federal Pell Grant
- Grants from your state
- Other scholarships?
- What you will be responsible for paying for
- Cost of attendance minus total grants and scholarships

Options to consider

- Work-study
- Loan options
- Family contributions
- Payment plans offered by the college
- Military benefits
- Non-federal private education loan

How do you know which college is the best deal?

First, consider the colleges individually. Did they offer aid? Was the aid offered competitive compared to the other colleges? Does this package make financial sense based on your child's desired career?

Second, compare each college side-by-side. Which college stands out as the best deal? If you are not happy with the financial package from one of your colleges, I recommend you appeal it using your other college offers as leverage. Determining the best college for your child is not always easy. You need to consider which college gave your child the most aid, excluding loans. This is what will allow your child to graduate with minimal debt in the least amount of time.

If you have exhausted all your options, here is what you will want to do to apply for financial aid:

Complete the Free Application for Federal Student Aid (FAFSA). The FAFSA calculates your student's eligibility for financial aid. Who should apply to the FAFSA? Every student who will be attending college should apply to the FAFSA. The most common response I get about FAFSA is, "Why should I apply for the FAFSA? I make too much money." What happens if your income changes tomorrow? Always have a plan B; it's like taking out college financial insurance. The second most popular question is, "What if I do not want to share my financial information?" The government already has your taxes. Your financial information is available to them. If you do not fill out the FAFSA, you are leaving potential money on the table.

If this all seems very confusing, you are not alone. You can either hire a professional to help you fill out your FAFSA, or you can pay someone to do it for you. We offer this service to our clients.

Where is all the free money:

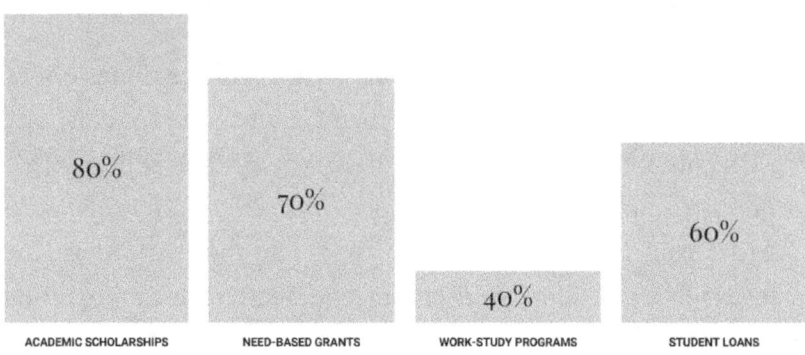

10 Secrets to Help You Find and Win Independent Scholarships

If you would like the most updated list, sign up for our newsletter, where I share new scholarships monthly at www.collegereadyplan.com.

Secret #1 – Most full-ride scholarships come from the college as a merit or athletic award. Once your child has been accepted to a college, look through that school's website for scholarship opportunities. Another option is to contact the college's financial aid office and ask how to find their scholarship applications and deadlines. Not every school will offer your child a scholarship, but it is worth asking.

Secret #2 – Following is a list of some of the biggest and most well-known private scholarships that offer substantial financial support to students:

1. The Gates Scholarship

Award	Full funding for college tuition, fees, room, board, and other expenses not covered by other financial aid.
Eligibility	High school seniors from low-income households who are minorities and demonstrate outstanding academic performance, leadership, and community service.
Details	Highly competitive, it aims to support 300 students each year.

2. Coca-Cola Scholars Program

Award	$20,000 scholarship for 150 high-achieving high school seniors.
Eligibility	U.S. high school seniors who demonstrate academic excellence, leadership, and community service.
Details	One of the most prestigious scholarships, focusing on well-rounded students.

3. Jack Kent Cooke Foundation Scholarship

Award	Up to $55,000 per year for up to four years, covering tuition, living expenses, books, and other required fees.
Eligibility	High-achieving high school seniors with financial need, including community college transfer students.
Details	One of the largest scholarships for students with exceptional academic records and significant financial need.

4. The Elks National Foundation Most Valuable Student Scholarship

Award	Ranges from $1,000 to $50,000.
Eligibility	High school seniors who demonstrate leadership, academic achievement, and community involvement.
Details	Awards are based on academic achievement, leadership, and financial need.

5. The Dell Scholars Program

Award	$20,000, a laptop, and access to ongoing support services.
Eligibility	Low-income, highly motivated students who demonstrate determination, grit, and financial need.
Details	Focuses on students who have overcome significant obstacles.

6. Horatio Alger Association Scholarship

Award	Up to $25,000.
Eligibility	High school seniors who demonstrate financial need, have overcome adversity, and are involved in extracurricular and community service activities.
Details	Supports students who have faced significant challenges in their lives.

7. QuestBridge National College Match Scholarship

Award	Full four-year scholarships to partner colleges, covering tuition, room, board, and other expenses.
Eligibility	High-achieving, low-income high school seniors who want to attend top colleges.
Details	Connects students with top universities, providing a path to a debt-free education.

8. Burger King Scholars Program

Award	Ranges from $1,000 to $50,000.
Eligibility	High school seniors and Burger King employees and their families with strong academic records and community involvement.
Details	Supports students pursuing higher education across a range of fields.

9. The Davidson Fellows Scholarship

Award	Ranges from $10,000 to $50,000.
Eligibility	Students 18 and under who have completed a significant project in science, technology, engineering, mathematics, literature, music, or philosophy.
Details	Recognizes and supports exceptionally gifted young people.

10. Ronald McDonald House Charities (RMHC) Scholarship

Award	Varies, typically ranging from $1,000 to $5,000.
Eligibility	High school seniors who have demonstrated academic achievement, leadership, and financial need.
Details	Provides multiple awards across various chapters nationwide.

11. GE-Reagan Foundation Scholarship

Award	$10,000 renewable for up to four years, totaling $40,000.
Eligibility	High school seniors who demonstrate leadership, drive, integrity, and citizenship.
Details	Named in honor of President Ronald Reagan, it rewards students who lead and serve in their communities.

12. Microsoft Imagine Cup Global Competition

Award	Up to $100,000 and mentorship opportunities.
Eligibility	Students with innovative technology projects that address global challenges.
Details	Open to students worldwide, it promotes innovation and creativity in technology.

13. Amazon Future Engineer Scholarship

Award	$40,000 plus a guaranteed paid internship at Amazon.
Eligibility	High school seniors planning to pursue a degree in computer science or a related field.
Details	Focuses on increasing access to computer science education for underrepresented students.

These scholarships are not only well-known for their generosity but also for their rigorous selection processes. They often consider academic performance, leadership qualities, financial need, and community involvement. Applying for these scholarships can be highly competitive, but they offer outstanding support to help students achieve their educational dreams.

Secret #4 – Look for scholarships from your employer, unions, or even your high school's PTA or PTC. There are some crazy ways to get awards. My daughter received one from her high school PTA because she was a Cheerleader all four years and in Leadership all four years. These scholarships are usually smaller, but they are quick and easy to apply to. The competition is smaller, and your chances of winning an award are greater. You may find these scholarships through your student's high school counseling office, local organizations like the Elks, Rotary Club, Lions Club, Knights of Columbus, local women's clubs, Masons, Optimists, Kiwanis, Jaycees, newspapers, or online.

Secret #5 – There are no tricks, but there is just good old hard work and follow through. Deadlines are critical. Directly and thoroughly answering the prompt for the essay is very important. Help your child realize that the scholarship application readers want to get to know them. They consider the following: What are your student's passions? What has your child accomplished? Why should your child receive this award over another student? What will increase your child's chances of winning? High GPA, test scores, class rank, community service hours, and leadership. Also, a strong essay will usually get the scholarship. I encourage all my students to take their time and have a professional edit the essay.

Secret #6 – Passion = Scholarships! Seek scholarships that your child has shown passion in, such as art, dance, theater, mock trials, leadership, community service, etc. It is important to highlight your child's unique talents or accomplishments.

Secret #7 – Consider your background. Many scholarships give money to students with particular ethnic or racial backgrounds. There are even scholarships for students in military families and students with parents in volunteer organizations and Greek societies. There are also a lot of scholarships designed for students who are returning to school late in life.

Secret #8 – If a scholarship advertises "no essay," do not waste your child's time applying. I have found that this is just a way to fish for your personal information and then sell it to other college lists like loan companies, etc.

Secret #9 – If your child does not go looking for a scholarship, it will not come to them. The chances of your child getting a private scholarship without researching and applying are 1%. On the flip side of that, your child could spend hundreds of hours researching and applying to private scholarships and get zero awards. There is no guarantee; it is a competition, and only the best application wins. Please keep in mind that if your child is chasing private scholarships and their grades drop, they may lose their chance to go to college.

Secret #10 – Have your child follow directions carefully. Answer each and every question. Do not assume the scholarship organization knows anything about your child. If there is a word count on the essay, adhere to it. If samples of your work are required, give them your best. Have someone double-check and proofread everything in the application. Build a spreadsheet to keep track of your deadlines!

What is the best type of scholarship your child can receive?

An 'Automatic Merit Scholarship' is awarded without you or your child having to do anything. The colleges have parameters regarding specific criteria like GPA or test scores, etc. This type of scholarship is used to get students to enroll at their college. These scholarships can be full tuition or a full ride (includes everything). Each college has different parameters, and a good College Consultant can lead you to the colleges that offer the most Automatic Merit Scholarships.

As a Certified College Admissions Strategist who has been helping families get into college and graduate with little to no debt, I have a list of the most generous colleges and the type of student they award most often. It is not something you can Google; it is knowledge I acquired over time by analyzing what schools give the best and most generous scholarships.

The Athletic Scholarship

Who gets a full ride? Full-ride athletic scholarships are incredibly rare, and only a small percentage of high school athletes receive them. Here's a breakdown of the reality behind full-ride athletic scholarships:

Percentage of High School Athletes Who Receive Athletic Scholarships

- Approximately **7% of high school athletes** go on to play sports at the college level (NCAA, NAIA, or NJCAA).

- Only about **2% of high school athletes** receive any form of athletic scholarship.

Percentage Receiving Full-Ride Scholarships

Full-ride athletic scholarships are typically reserved for high-profile sports like football, basketball, and sometimes women's volleyball, tennis, and gymnastics.

For NCAA Division I schools, the sports that generally offer full-ride scholarships are "headcount sports" (like football and basketball), where scholarships are not divided among players.

> **Only about 1% or less of high school athletes receive a full-ride athletic scholarship to any college.**

Most athletic scholarships are partial, covering only a portion of the costs, such as tuition, fees, books, or room and board.

Many college athletes are on partial scholarships that require families to cover the remaining costs of attendance.

Success in securing an athletic scholarship often depends not just on athletic ability but also on academic performance, as maintaining eligibility requires meeting specific academic standards.

Given the competitiveness, aspiring student-athletes should also focus on academics and seek other forms of financial aid and scholarships to complement any potential athletic money.

Studying Abroad

If you are looking for a nontraditional US college opportunity, you will want to check out our latest addition to College Ready. University Ready was started in 2022 when my stepdaughter decided she did not want to follow her oldest brother to Harvard, her oldest sister to the University of Alabama, or her other brother to San Francisco State University. She wanted to study international business, become an entrepreneur, and graduate debt-free like her older siblings.

After endless hours of research, we presented the idea of studying in Europe to her protective father. He listened with an open mind but had many concerns. As a family, we created a plan to prepare her for her dream of studying in Europe. Not only did she meet all 20 expectations/goals, but she was also more than prepared to study in Europe. With her father's blessing, we dropped her off at her new home for the next three years.

She will graduate this spring with a dual US and European Business degree. We spent a total of $27,000, and she experienced living internationally. If you believe this would be a great option for your child or maybe just doing one year abroad, I would be happy to help you navigate this unique opportunity. You will find information on University Ready by going to our website, www.collegereadyplan.com.

Quick PLAN for Parents

For those busy parents who do not have time to read the entire book

P = PLAN for Your Child's Academic Positioning
....

- Who will create your child's stand-out strategy?

- Who will create a plan for positioning? What do you want colleges to know about your child?

- Has your child taken the most challenging classes available to him or her?

- Is the IB program worth transferring high schools for? Is IB or AP a better fit for your child's success?

- Does your child's high school offer Dual enrollment? Is it the right fit for them?

- Who will determine what GPA your child will need to get into their dream school? Is it realistic?

- Is your child a strong test taker? Will he or she be an AP Scholar?

- How will you determine if the PSAT/SAT/ACT/AP test scores are needed? How many times should your child take each test, and when should they take them?

- Will your child's PSAT score qualify them to be a National Merit Scholar?

- Have you created a timeline that is specific and measurable? Will your child follow it?

- Do you have a plan A, B and C? One teacher, subject, or injury can change the entire plan.

L = LEARN What Your Child Is Passionate About

- Who will determine your child's passions, talents, and the qualities that make him or her stand out? What tools will you use? Have you started the conversation with your child?

- What are your child's areas of opportunity? How will you help them overcome those challenges?

- What will colleges remember about your child?

- Does your child know how to collaborate with others regardless of their diversity and beliefs?

- Have you logged all your child's community service hours? Have they been signed off by a qualified certifier?

- Does your child's community service project tell the college something about your child?

- Have they won local, regional, national, and international awards for something they are passionate about?

- Can they write an essay about what matters most to them or who they will advocate for?

- Are they prepared to share what they have done in an interview?

- Will they start their own service project? How will they accomplish this, and when will they do it?

A = APPLYING TO COLLEGE: The Application, Leadership, Extracurriculars, Recommenders and Essays

- Who will create your child's academic plan to help them stand out?

- Who will pick the list of colleges they will apply to? How many schools?

- Who will choose if a college is a reach, comfort, or safety school?

- How many AP/IB/Dual Enrollment/College classes will your child need to stand out on their applications? Is this course load realistic?

- Do you have a plan for who will review every application?

LEADERSHIP

- Has your child received leadership recognition or awards?

- Have they been voted into office, lead in a play, or captain of their sport?

- Has your child led other students who are older or younger than he or she is?

- Has your child been the founder of something important to them? Have they led others to create change?

- Has your child led others in student government, yearbook, sport, band, etc.?

EXTRACURRICULARS

- Who will oversee keeping a list of all extracurricular activities your child has been involved in since they were promoted from middle school?

- Does your child's extracurriculars tell colleges something about them?

- Will your child play a sport in college? Do they have video footage to share? Are they local, state, or nationally ranked? Do they know the rules of engagement?

- Will your child apply as an artist? Does your child have an up-to-date art portfolio? Have they won awards?

- Who will create a resume highlighting all their activities, honors, and awards? Who will put it in the correct order? Who will polish it?

RECOMMENDERS

- How will you choose who will be the people your child asks to write their letters of recommendation?

- Will you forfeit your right to see the letters of recommendation before they are submitted to the college?

- How many recommenders will you ask? How will you ask them, and when?

- If applying to a military academy, do you know the exact recommenders needed?

- Does your child know how to have a successful interview? Who will help them craft their questions and answers?

ESSAYS

- Does your child have enough experience to write between 5-18 essays per college without talking about the same experience twice?

- Who will help your child pick the essay prompt to write about, and who will determine if it is the best option to help them stand out?

- Who will help your child brainstorm, outline, and strategize the essays?

- How will you keep track of each essay needed and written for each application? Who will track the deadlines?

- Will you be the final editor, or will you hire a professional?

Below is the full set of current essay prompts:

1. Some students have a background, identity, interest, or talent that is so meaningful they believe their application would be incomplete without it. If this sounds like you, then please share your story.

2. The lessons we take from obstacles we encounter can be fundamental to later success. Recount a time when you faced a challenge, setback, or failure. How did it affect you, and what did you learn from the experience?

3. Reflect on a time when you questioned or challenged a belief or idea. What prompted your thinking? What was the outcome?

4. Reflect on something that someone has done for you that has made you happy or thankful in a surprising way. How has this gratitude affected or motivated you?

5. Discuss an accomplishment, event, or realization that sparked a period of personal growth and a new understanding of yourself or others.

6. Describe a topic, idea, or concept you find so engaging that it makes you lose all track of time. Why does it captivate you? What or who do you turn to when you want to learn more?

7. Share an essay on any topic of your choice. It can be one you've already written, one that responds to a different prompt, or one of your own design.

Can your child write essays on at least four of the topics listed above?

N = Negotiate: College is a Business – Do Not Pay Full Price

- Have you looked for colleges with strong merit scholarships?

- Can your family afford college? Can your child afford not to get a college degree?

- Have you started saving for college? Are you saving your money in the best asset? Do you know what the FAFSA looks at and what they do not?

- Have you calculated your SAI, FAFSA, and CSS Profile? Have you estimated your cost of attendance?

- Do you know all your options? Which grants, scholarships, work-study, and federal loans will you be eligible for?

- Will your child graduate in 4 years?

- Have you looked for out-of-state public colleges or international schools with special pricing for out-of-state students?

- Have you looked for private schools that meet 100% of need?

- Decide whether your child's desired college is a want or a need.

- Who will research and apply for the best scholarships for your child?

- How will you compare award letters?

- Who will request your financial reconsideration? Lead the financial negotiation?

Final Thoughts

I recommend you keep this book with you throughout the planning process. Refer to it often to make sure your PLAN is in place and your child's strategy is in alignment with their goals and dreams.

It is my hope that you found this book valuable. I wrote this book because my desire is that you enjoy the last four years with your child at home full-time. If you believe this book will help another parent and child, please spread the word to others, write a review of it on Amazon, or buy a book and be a hero to a friend. Having reviews helps people who are deciding whether to purchase the book decide. Reviews are not easy to get, so if you could take a few minutes to write one, I would really appreciate it. Please visit Amazon.com now to write a review.

Next Steps

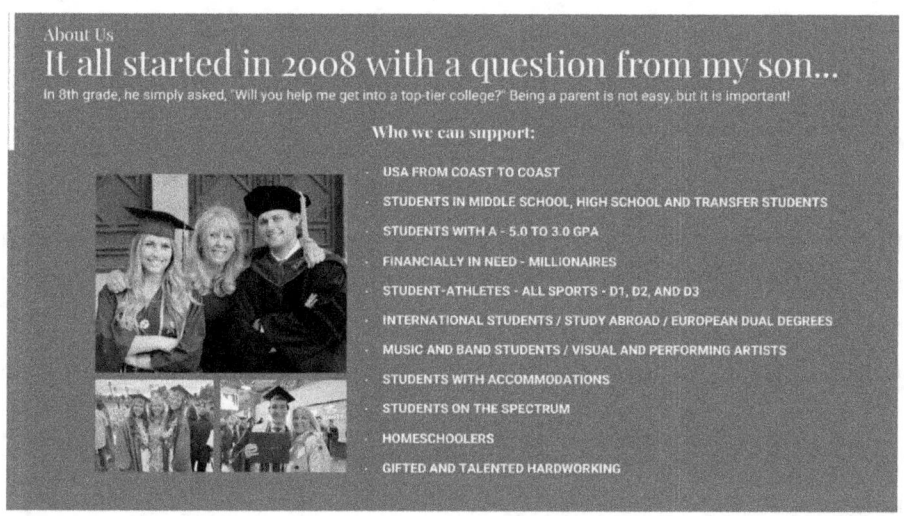

If you are still overwhelmed and do not want to figure this out on your own, I have another option. I created the College Ready Plan for families like yours.

Our program is unique—there's nothing else like it in the world. I developed this program based on my success with my own children, and over the past 17 years, we've replicated this success with thousands of students. Our comprehensive, personalized plan is designed to maximize your child's potential while minimizing stress and financial burden.

We begin by crafting a personalized "Stand-Out Strategy." We develop a tailored plan highlighting your child's unique strengths and aspirations. This detailed roadmap ensures they are positioned to stand out in a crowded applicant pool, capturing the attention of admissions officers.

Understanding the demands on your family's time, we offer **convenient online meetings** tailored to your schedule. We record every session so you can revisit our discussions whenever it's convenient for you, ensuring you never miss valuable information. After each student meeting, we provide updates to parents—you can choose to be as involved as you like or entrust us to manage the process on your behalf.

Our program includes **regular check-ins** to keep your child motivated and on track. We host weekly "Passion with Purpose" meetings that inspire and guide students in developing meaningful projects and monthly small group sessions, where we foster a sense of community and shared learning. Our quarterly essay writing workshops hone their storytelling skills and create a plan for their future essays. Additionally, we offer custom one-on-one meetings with professional certified consultants to address specific needs and goals.

Beyond individualized support, we provide access to **exclusive resources and a supportive community**. You'll be invited to private monthly webinars where we share the most up-to-date information on college admissions. Our monthly client newsletters and urgent text updates ensure you're always informed about important developments. Joining our private social media group connects you with other families on the same journey, offering weekly updates, insights, and a platform to get your questions answered promptly.

We recognize that **time management and organization** are crucial skills for success. That's why we dedicate time to helping your child develop these abilities, recommending tools and tips to keep them organized and focused. Our goal is to empower them not just academically but also personally, fostering habits that will benefit them throughout college and beyond.

When it comes to navigating the competitive landscape of college admissions, a well-crafted academic strategy is paramount. **It all begins with a Personalized Academic Roadmap tailored specifically to your child's goals and aspirations.**

We start by conducting a thorough **Transcript and Report Card Evaluation.** Each semester, we review your child's current performance, celebrating successes and identifying areas for improvement. Based on this analysis, we make strategic recommendations for future classes that align with their interests and the expectations of top-tier colleges.

No matter where your family is in the journey—whether your child is in middle school, a freshman just starting high school or a junior gearing up for applications—we develop a **comprehensive Academic Plan** customized to your needs. This plan is not just a schedule of classes; it's a dynamic roadmap that outlines a rigorous academic path with built-in backup options to ensure college readiness. We anticipate potential challenges and adapt as needed so your child remains on track toward their goals.

Understanding that grades are a critical component of college applications, we perform a detailed **GPA Evaluation.** Here, we identify strategies to enhance your child's academic standing, such as weighted courses, honors classes, Advanced Placement, Dual Enrollment, or College options that can boost their GPA and demonstrate their commitment to academic excellence.

An often-overlooked aspect of college preparation is the **A-G Evaluation.** Colleges, especially those in the University of California system, require students to complete specific courses in designated categories. Missing even one can limit your child's college options. We meticulously ensure that all necessary coursework is completed in the right order so no opportunities are missed due to administrative oversight.

But academics are only part of the equation. Finding the right college fit is crucial for your child's happiness and success. That's why we offer **College Matching and Exploration** services. I developed our proprietary **College Match Strategy**—the very same one I used to help my own son gain admission to Harvard. This strategy considers academic, social, and financial factors to identify colleges where your child will thrive both in and out of the classroom.

To bring these options to life, we assist with **College Tour Planning**. Visiting campuses can be transformative, providing firsthand insights that brochures and websites can't capture. We guide you on when to visit, which schools to prioritize, and how to make the most of each tour experience. Additionally, we teach your child how to show **demonstrated interest**, a factor that many colleges consider during the admissions process.

We understand that planning these visits can be time-consuming and costly. That's why we've developed **Custom Templates** to streamline the process, saving your family both time and money. These templates include recommendations, questions for campus representatives, and checklists to ensure you gather all the information you need.

Enhancing your child's academic profile doesn't stop at selecting the right courses. We provide **Coursework Recommendations** to help your child stand out. This includes navigating options like dual enrollment programs, where they can take college-level classes while still in high school, and identifying other opportunities that align with their interests and enhance their transcripts.

Should academic challenges arise, we offer **Tutoring Recommendations**. Recognizing that every student has unique needs, we develop personalized plans to address any areas where your child may need extra support. Our network of experienced tutors specializes in a variety of subjects and learning styles, ensuring that your child receives the assistance they need to excel.

Finally, we help your child present their achievements professionally through our **Resume Building Software**. A compelling resume is a valuable tool not only for college applications but also for securing internships, scholarships, and mentorship opportunities. We guide your child in highlighting their strengths, experiences, and accomplishments in a way that resonates with admissions committees and recommenders.

In essence, our academic strategy is about more than just getting your child into college; it's about fostering a journey of self-discovery, growth, and preparedness that will serve them well beyond their university years. With personalized guidance and a strategic approach, we aim to make the path to college a rewarding and confidence-building experience for your entire family.

Navigating the landscape of standardized testing can be a significant source of stress for students and their families. Questions like "Which test should my child take?" or "When is the best time to test?" often arise, adding confusion to an already complex process. That's why we offer a comprehensive **Test Strategy** designed to demystify standardized tests and empower your child to perform at their best.

Our approach begins with a **Comprehensive Testing Plan** tailored specifically to your child's needs. Understanding the differences between the SAT and ACT is crucial, but more importantly, we focus on identifying which test aligns best with your child's strengths. This isn't mere guesswork; we use real numbers and thorough analysis to make this determination.

To achieve this, we provide **Custom Timed Diagnostic Tests** for both the SAT and ACT. These full-length exams replicate the actual testing environment, allowing your child to experience each test under realistic conditions. After the diagnostics, we conduct in-depth evaluations of the results. This analysis highlights areas of strength and opportunities for improvement, giving us valuable insights into which test is the better fit.

With the preferred test identified, we offer **Test Prep and Strategy Recommendations** that connect your child with top-tier test prep resources and strategists. Recognizing that every student has unique learning preferences and that families have different budgets and schedules, we provide a range of options. Whether it's free resources, group classes, or personalized one-to-one tutoring, we help you select the best fit for your child's preparation.

Timing is a critical factor in standardized testing success, which is why we create a **Customized Timeline** for your child. We'll guide you on when to register for tests, considering factors like application deadlines, academic workload, and extracurricular commitments. Knowing when and where to test removes uncertainty and ensures your child is adequately prepared on test day.

We spend time setting clear, achievable score goals based on the admissions criteria of your child's target schools. Understanding the scores needed for these institutions provides motivation and a concrete objective to work toward. This clarity transforms the testing process from a daunting challenge into a series of manageable steps.

Our comprehensive test strategy not only aims to improve your child's test scores but also to reduce stress and build confidence. By combining personalized assessments with expert recommendations and strategic planning, we turn standardized testing into an opportunity for your child to shine.

Throughout this journey, we're here to support your family every step of the way. Our goal is to make standardized testing a positive and empowering experience that complements your child's academic achievements and strengthens their college applications. With our guidance, your child can approach test day with confidence, knowing they have the tools and preparation to succeed.

Developing leadership skills and engaging in meaningful extracurricular activities are pivotal in crafting a standout college application. Our comprehensive **Leadership Strategy** is designed to nurture your child's innate abilities and provide them with opportunities to shine as influential leaders. There are many types of leaders, and we help your child find their leadership opportunities.

We begin by offering the opportunity to earn four prestigious Leadership Certifications. These certifications are more than just accolades; they represent a commitment to personal growth and the ability to inspire and guide others. Through targeted programs and mentorship, your child will develop essential leadership skills such as effective communication, strategic planning, and team collaboration. These certifications serve as tangible evidence of their leadership capabilities, making a strong impression on college admissions committees.

Understanding the importance of global perspectives in today's interconnected world, we provide chances to hold **International Leadership Positions.** Your child can engage in roles that demonstrate global impact, such as participating in our international service project. This not only broadens their worldview but also showcases their ability to lead initiatives that transcend borders, reflecting a commitment to making a difference on a global scale.

To ensure your child stays on track, we implement a **Leadership Timeline,** which includes a points system based on what colleges are looking for in applicants. This structured approach helps your child set goals, monitor progress, and focus on experiences that will enhance their leadership profile. By aligning their efforts with the expectations of top-tier institutions, we maximize their potential for acceptance into their desired colleges.

In addition to leadership development, our **Extracurricular Strategy** focuses on maximizing your child's activities and honors to create a compelling and holistic application. We start with an **Activities Evaluation**, meticulously polishing and ranking their extracurriculars, honors, and awards. The Common Application allows only ten activity slots, and the UC Application allows 20. Without a strategic plan, it's challenging to fill these spots effectively. We help your child prioritize and present their experiences in a way that highlights their passions and achievements.

Our **Stand-Out Strategy** involves positioning your child's experiences to emphasize their uniqueness. We work closely with them to identify what sets them apart—be it a rare skill, a unique hobby, or an unconventional accomplishment—and ensure this is clearly communicated in their application. This tailored approach makes their profile memorable to admissions officers who sift through thousands of applications.

We also provide access to a wealth of **Opportunities and Experiences** to further enhance their application:

- **Research Opportunities**: We assist in securing meaningful research projects, allowing your child to contribute to academic fields they are passionate about. Engaging in research demonstrates intellectual curiosity and a commitment to advancing knowledge.

- **Internship Opportunities**: We guide your child in finding and securing internships that offer real-world experience and professional growth. Internships provide practical skills and insights that are highly valued by colleges.

- **Business Building**: For entrepreneurial spirits, we support your child in developing their own business ventures. This showcases initiative, creativity, and the ability to drive projects from concept to execution.

- **Summer Strategy**: We offer recommendations and share examples of past students' successful summer plans. Whether it's attending specialized programs, volunteering, or pursuing personal projects, we help your child make the most of their summer break to further their goals.

Central to our approach is fostering a **Passion with Purpose Project**. We believe that community service should be more than just a checkbox—it should be a meaningful endeavor that reflects your child's values and interests. Our **Passion with Purpose Masterclass** is an online course that guides your child step-by-step in developing a community service project that aligns with their passions. This not only benefits the community but also provides a profound personal growth experience.

Through this initiative, your child has the opportunity for **National Recognition**, with the opportunity to earn eight national awards. Such accolades significantly enhance their college applications, demonstrating dedication, leadership, and impact.

We also encourage **International Participation**, engaging in global initiatives that broaden perspectives and showcase a willingness to contribute on a worldwide scale.

To bring their vision to life, we offer **Project Development** assistance. Starting and leading a community service project can be daunting, but with our support, your child will navigate this process confidently. From concept to implementation, we guide them in creating a project that makes a genuine difference and reflects their commitment to making our world a better place.

By intertwining leadership development, strategic extracurricular planning, and purposeful community engagement, we equip your child with a robust and compelling profile. Our holistic approach ensures that every aspect of their application tells a story of a well-rounded, passionate, and proactive individual ready to contribute meaningfully to their future college community and beyond.

With our dedicated support, your child won't just be preparing an application—they'll be embarking on a journey of personal growth, leadership, and impactful experiences that will serve them well into their college years and future endeavors.

Crafting a compelling college application is both an art and a science. Beyond grades and test scores, it's the essays and letters of recommendation that breathe life into an application, revealing the person behind the achievements. Our holistic approach to the **Essay Strategy** and **Recommender Strategy** ensures that your child's unique voice is heard and their strengths are highlighted effectively.

Our Essay Strategy is designed to guide your child in creating powerful, authentic essays that resonate with admissions committees. We believe in the importance of Early Introduction to the essay-writing process. That's why, at your child's very first meeting with us, we'll share the essay prompts they'll be tackling. This early start allows them ample time to reflect on their experiences, brainstorm ideas, and avoid the last-minute rush that can hinder creativity and clarity.

To support your child in this journey, we provide access to **Top Essay Editors** who are seasoned professionals in the field of college admissions. These editors offer valuable feedback, helping your child refine their narratives, enhance their writing style, and ensure their essays are both compelling and true to their voice.

Understanding that inspiration often comes from collaboration, we host **Brainstorming Workshops** on a quarterly basis. These interactive sessions are designed to inspire ideas and help students discover unique angles for their essays. Through group discussions and individual exercises, your child can explore different themes and storytelling techniques, fostering creativity and confidence in their writing.

We also equip your child with **Essay Building Tools** that transform their resumes and life experiences into powerful stories. By connecting their accomplishments and activities to personal growth and future aspirations, they learn to craft essays that are not just lists of achievements but narratives that highlight their journey and character.

Managing multiple essays for different colleges can be overwhelming. Our **Organized Approach** includes an online essay organizer and timeline, allowing your child to keep track of prompts, deadlines, and progress all in one place. This system ensures they stay on top of their work, reduce stress, and allocate adequate time to each essay for maximum impact.

Complementing strong essays and securing impactful letters of recommendation is crucial. Our **Recommender Strategy** is focused on helping your child obtain endorsements that genuinely reflect their abilities and potential.

We begin with **Strategic Planning**, guiding your child on when and who to ask for letters of recommendation. Timing is key—we ensure they approach their recommenders well in advance, giving these individuals ample time to craft thoughtful and detailed letters. We help identify teachers, mentors, or supervisors who have witnessed your child's growth and can speak passionately about their strengths.

Understanding the nuances of making such requests, we provide guidance on the **Approach and Follow-Up**. Your child will learn how to professionally and respectfully ask for recommendations, provide necessary context, and politely remind recommenders as deadlines approach. This not only secures strong endorsements but also teaches valuable interpersonal skills.

To facilitate the process further, we focus on **Providing Resources** to the recommenders. We assist your child in preparing a comprehensive packet that may include their resume, a summary of accomplishments, specific anecdotes, and any prompts or guidelines provided by the colleges. By ensuring that recommenders have all the information they need, we help them write letters that are detailed, personalized, and aligned with application requirements.

By integrating these strategies, we aim to highlight your child's unique story and present a cohesive, compelling application. Our goal is not just to get them into college but to empower them with skills and confidence that will serve them throughout their academic and professional lives.

With our dedicated support, your child will:

- **Express their authentic voice** through essays that captivate and inspire.

- **Stand out** with personalized recommendations that underscore their strengths.

- **Stay organized and confident** throughout the application process.

We're committed to making this journey as enriching and stress-free as possible, providing the tools, expertise, and encouragement your child needs to succeed. Together, we'll turn the often, overwhelming task of college applications into an opportunity for growth and self-discovery, paving the way for their future success.

Navigating the financial aspects of college planning can be one of the most challenging and stressful parts of the admissions process. Understanding how to maximize financial aid opportunities while minimizing out-of-pocket expenses is crucial for families aiming to make higher education affordable. That's why we've developed a comprehensive **Financial Strategy** designed to guide you through every step of this complex journey.

Our approach begins with demystifying the financial aid process and empowering your family with knowledge and tools to make informed decisions. At the core of this strategy is the calculation of your family's Student Aid Index (SAI). Formerly known as the Expected Family Contribution (EFC), the SAI is a number used by colleges to determine how much each college thinks your family should be able to pay. We help you calculate your family's SAI, providing a clear picture of how colleges assess your ability to pay for education. Understanding this figure is crucial, as it influences the types and amounts of aid your child may be offered.

But we don't stop at calculation. We **explore ways to potentially lower your SAI**, which can increase your eligibility for scholarships and grants. By examining your financial situation, we identify strategies such as asset reallocation, timing of income, and other financial planning techniques that may legally and ethically reduce your SAI, thereby enhancing your aid opportunities. We show you what is on the FAFSA and what is not considered.

Navigating the Free Application for Federal Student Aid (FAFSA) and the CSS Profile can be daunting, as mistakes or omissions can lead to reduced aid offers or delays in processing. We provide **comprehensive guidance on understanding and correctly completing these critical forms**. Our expertise ensures that your applications are accurate and submitted on time, maximizing your chances of receiving the best possible financial aid package.

Once financial aid offers start rolling in, comparing them can be confusing. Each college may present its package differently, with various combinations of grants, loans, work-study opportunities, and scholarships. We help **analyze and compare financial aid offers**, helping you decipher the details and understand the true cost of each option. With our insights, we can tell you whether you've received a fair, good, or great offer, empowering you to make the best financial decision for your family.

If an aid offer doesn't meet your needs or expectations, know that you have options. We provide **support in negotiations and reconsiderations**, guiding you through the process of appealing for better financial packages. Drawing on our experience and knowledge of college policies and past offers, we help you craft effective appeals that can lead to increased aid and reduced costs.

Our commitment to your family's financial well-being extends beyond immediate aid offers. We focus on long-term strategies to help your child graduate debt-free or with minimal debt.

Through our **Debt-Free Planning**, you'll gain access to the **College Ready Debt-Free Plan**, a comprehensive roadmap designed to minimize or eliminate college debt.

Recognizing that financial literacy is an essential life skill, we offer a **Financial Literacy Certification** for your child. This program equips them with fundamental knowledge about budgeting, managing expenses, understanding credit, and making informed financial decisions. By fostering financial responsibility early on, we prepare your child not only for college but for a lifetime of sound financial management. This will help them to make the best college decision.

Choosing the right college can significantly impact your financial obligations. We provide a curated **List of the Most Generous Colleges**, identifying institutions known for substantial aid and favorable financial packages. By considering these schools, your child may have access to higher levels of scholarships and grants, reducing the overall cost of education.

In essence, our Financial Strategy is about more than just securing aid; it's about empowering your family with knowledge, resources, and support to make the best financial decisions.

With our guidance, you will:

- **Understand how colleges determine your financial need**, giving you clarity and control over the process.

- **Identify opportunities to increase aid eligibility**, maximizing the financial support your child receives.

- **Navigate critical financial aid applications** with confidence and accuracy, avoiding common pitfalls.

- **Make informed comparisons of financial aid offers**, ensuring you choose the option that best fits your family's needs.

- **Effectively negotiate for better financial packages**, potentially reducing your out-of-pocket costs.

- **Plan strategically to minimize or eliminate college debt**, setting your child up for financial success post-graduation.

- **Equip your child with essential financial literacy skills**, fostering independence and responsible money management.

- **Explore colleges known for generous aid**, broadening options that align with both educational goals and financial considerations.

We understand that the prospect of financing a college education can be overwhelming, but you don't have to navigate it alone. Our expertise and personalized approach turn a complex process into a manageable and even empowering experience. We're here to advocate for your family's best interests, ensuring that financial constraints don't stand in the way of your child's educational aspirations.

Together, we'll work towards a future where your child can pursue their dreams without the burden of excessive debt, confident in the knowledge that they've made wise financial choices supported by a dedicated team of professionals.

Navigating the final year of high school can be both exhilarating and overwhelming for students and their families. It's a time filled with important decisions, deadlines, and the anticipation of embarking on a new chapter of life. Our **Senior Year Support** is meticulously designed to ensure that your child is not only prepared but also confident and excited about the journey ahead.

Achieving Application Success is a central focus of our support strategy.

We start by developing a comprehensive **Application Strategy and Timeline** tailored to your child's unique goals and target colleges. This clear plan outlines every step of the application process, from gathering necessary documents to crafting compelling essays, ensuring that your child stays ahead of deadlines and avoids last-minute stress. By having a structured timeline, they can manage their workload effectively and focus on presenting their best selves to admissions committees.

Selecting a major is a significant decision that can shape your child's academic experience and future career path. Our **Major Selection and Guidance** offers personalized support in choosing a field of study that aligns with their passions, strengths, and career aspirations.

We delve into strategies tailored for each college, considering factors like program reputation, faculty expertise, and available resources. This thoughtful approach helps your child make informed decisions that resonate with their long-term objectives.

Interviews are often a pivotal component of the college admissions process, providing an opportunity for your child to showcase their personality, enthusiasm, and suitability for the institution. We offer comprehensive **Interview Preparation**, including live mock interviews and personalized coaching. Through these sessions, your child gains valuable experience, receives constructive feedback, and builds the confidence needed to make a lasting positive impression during actual interviews.

In the competitive landscape of college admissions, being placed on a waitlist can be disheartening, but it's not the end of the road. Our **Waitlist Strategies** equip your child with techniques to improve their chances of acceptance if waitlisted. We guide them in crafting persuasive letters of continued interest, updating admissions offices with new achievements, and demonstrating sustained enthusiasm for the school. These proactive steps can significantly enhance their prospects of moving off the waitlist.

Sometimes, circumstances arise that make immediate college enrollment challenging or reconsideration necessary. In such cases, we provide **Deferral Guidance** to support your child in making the best decision. Whether they're considering a gap year to explore personal interests, gain work experience, or address unforeseen challenges, we help them navigate the deferral process smoothly. We ensure they understand the implications and requirements so they can make choices that align with their personal growth and future plans.

Preparing for college is not just about gaining admission; it's also about laying the foundation for a fulfilling and sustainable career. Our **Career and Assessments** services are designed to help your child explore their interests, understand the evolving job market, and make strategic decisions about their future.

We begin with **Comprehensive Assessments** that delve into your child's strengths, personality traits, and aptitudes. Using proven assessment tools, we help them gain insights into which careers may be the best fit. This self-awareness is crucial for selecting a major and career path that will be both rewarding and aligned with their natural abilities and interests.

Building on these insights, we facilitate **Career Exploration** discussions that broaden their understanding of potential professions. We provide recommendations and engage in conversations about various industries, job roles, and the education or training required for each. This exploration helps your child envision different possibilities and identify paths that excite them.

In today's rapidly changing world, it's essential to consider **Real-World Considerations** that could impact future employment. We address thought-provoking questions like, "Will a robot be doing your job in five years?" By examining trends in automation, artificial intelligence, and industry disruptions, we help your child understand which careers are likely to remain in demand and offer long-term stability. This forward-thinking approach ensures they are preparing for a future where their skills will be valued.

Financial implications are another critical aspect of career planning. We tackle important questions such as, "If you go into college debt, how long will it take to pay it off?" By analyzing potential salaries in various fields, the cost of education, and the return on investment, we provide a realistic perspective on how different career choices can affect financial well-being. This information empowers your child to make decisions that balance their passions with practical considerations about income and debt management.

Our holistic approach is designed to support your child not just academically but also personally and professionally. With our **Senior Year Support**, they will navigate the college application process with confidence and clarity. Through **Career and Assessments**, they will gain valuable insights that set the stage for long-term success and fulfillment.

By choosing our program, your child will benefit from:

- **Personalized Planning**: Tailored strategies that align with their unique goals and aspirations.

- **Expert Guidance**: Access to experienced professionals who provide mentorship and advice.

- **Confidence Building**: Tools and support that enhance self-assurance in interviews and decision-making.

- **Strategic Positioning**: Techniques to stand out in the admissions process, even in challenging situations like waitlisting.

- **Future-Focused Insights**: Understanding of market trends and financial considerations that influence career choices.

We are committed to being partners in your child's journey, providing the resources and support they need to turn their college dreams into reality and lay the groundwork for a bright and prosperous future.

It is my hope that by sharing what we do to help our families be successful, you will be inspired to do all of this with your child or choose to get the support you need. **We offer plans starting at $497 that can help you get what you want and need.**

Using the PLAN strategy, your child will simplify the college admissions process, reduce the overwhelm, and have an opportunity to graduate debt-free.

Glossary

ACT (American College Testing): is a college admission test based on English, Math, Social Studies, Reading Skills, and Scientific Reasoning.

AP (Advanced Placement Program): The College Board allows students to take college-level courses while in high school. If the student scores high enough on the national exam, college credit may be granted for the course.

Award Letter: The document you receive from the college you have been accepted into and what that college is offering you financially.

CLEP (College Level Exam Program): allows testing for possible college credit for beginning college courses.

College Credit: Passing the course counts towards a college degree.

Common Application: Several colleges use this application for admittance.

Cost of Attendance: The total expenses before financial aid.

Dual Enrollment: While students are enrolled in high school, they may take a college-level class at the same time. Often taught by a high school teacher at their high school. It is ENROLLMENT STATUS based on the number of credit hours you have taken.

Extra-Curricular Activities: Students do outside of normal classroom courses.

FAFSA (Free Application for Federal Student Financial Aid): The form that must be completed by the family to determine the family's expected contribution.

Financial Aid: The money given to students to help pay for college, such as Grants, loans, and scholarships.

529 Savings Plan: A state-sponsored investment plan to help families save money for college (we do not recommend this plan)

Grant: Financial aid that does not have to be paid back.

Honors Program: An opportunity for students to take challenging high school classes.

IB (International Baccalaureate Program): This program is only available at high schools that have qualified to offer it. It allows college-level subject area curriculum based on global interpretation.

Loan: Money you borrow that must be paid back with interest.

Merit Aid: Financial aid awarded to students based on their personal achievements.

NAIA (National Association of Intercollegiate Athletes): An association that governs communication between college coaches and student players at small schools.

NCAA (National Collegiate Athletic Association): An association that governs communication between college coaches and student players at large schools.

Need-Based Financial Aid: Financial aid given to students because they and their families cannot pay the full cost of attending.

Need-Blind Admission: College admission decision without the knowledge of the applicant's financial situation.

Net Price: The true amount a student will pay for college.

Net Price Calculator: An online tool that gives you a personalized estimate of what it will cost to attend a specific college.

NSCAA (National Small College Athletic Association): An association that governs communication between college coaches and student players at very small schools.

Outside Scholarship: A private scholarship offered by a private organization, not the government or college.

Priority Date: The date by which your application must be received to be given the best consideration.

Reserve Officers' Training Corps (ROTC): Offered by the military and available at some colleges that offer scholarships to students who agree to serve in the military after they graduate.

Residency Requirements: the amount of time a student has to live in a state before he or she is eligible for in-state tuition.

Student Aid Report (SAR): The report sent to families after they submit the FAFSA, which explains what the SAI is.

FREE GIFT FOR MY READERS

Is Your Teen Ready?

Do you find your child uncertain about their passions or future goals? Are they struggling to craft a compelling college essay? Can they clearly express what makes them stand out in a college interview? Often, they just don't know where to begin. That's where I come in. This is a gift for middle and high school students.

MY GIFT TO YOUR TEEN

I am on a mission to inspire teenagers worldwide. Every week, I personally meet with teenagers on Zoom to help them find what they are passionate about, create the change they want to see in the world, and step into leadership roles.

If your teen is ready to develop a standout strategy for college admissions, earn meaningful service hours, or learn to lead their peers in making impactful changes, simply scan the QR code to register. We'll send you the Zoom link to join this transformative journey! There is no cost to your family.

If you have questions or need clarification about your child's strategy, go to www.collegereadyplan.info